How to Open & Operate a Financially Successful

RETAIL

Business

With Companion CD-ROM

By Janet Engle

HOW TO OPEN & OPERATE A FINANCIALLY SUCCESSFUL
RETAIL BUSINESS — WITH COMPANION CD-ROM

Copyright © 2007 by Atlantic Publishing Group, Inc.
1405 SW 6th Ave. • Ocala, Florida 34471 • 800-814-1132 • 352-622-1875–Fax
Web site: www.atlantic-pub.com • E-mail: sales@atlantic-pub.com
SAN Number: 268-1250

ISBN-13: 978-1-60138-116-3   ISBN-10: 1-60138-116-6

Library of Congress Cataloging-in-Publication Data

Engle, Janet.
  How to open & operate a financially successful retail business : with companion
CD-ROM / by Janet Engle.
    p. cm.
  ISBN-13: 978-1-60138-116-3 (alk. paper)
  ISBN-10: 1-60138-116-6 (alk. paper)
  1. Retail trade--Ownership. 2. Franchises (Retail trade) 3. New business enterpris-es--Management. I. Title. II. Title: How to open and operate a financially successful retail business.

  HF5429.E4557 2007
  658.8'7--dc22

                    2007025042

Printed on Recycled Paper

EDITOR: Tracie Kendziora • tkendziora@atlantic-pub.com
PROOFREADER: Vickie Taylor • vtaylor@atlantic-pub.com

Printed in the United States

We recently lost our beloved pet "Bear," who was not only our best and dearest friend but also the "Vice President of Sunshine" here at Atlantic Publishing. He did not receive a salary but worked tirelessly 24 hours a day to please his parents. Bear was a rescue dog that turned around and showered myself, my wife Sherri, his grandparents Jean, Bob and Nancy and every person and animal he met (maybe not rabbits) with friendship and love. He made a lot of people smile every day.

We wanted you to know that a portion of the profits of this book will be donated to The Humane Society of the United States. –*Douglas & Sherri Brown*

The human-animal bond is as old as human history. We cherish our animal companions for their unconditional affection and acceptance. We feel a thrill when we glimpse wild creatures in their natural habitat or in our own backyard.

Unfortunately, the human-animal bond has at times been weakened. Humans have exploited some animal species to the point of extinction.

The Humane Society of the United States makes a difference in the lives of animals here at home and worldwide. The HSUS is dedicated to creating a world where our relationship with animals is guided by compassion. We seek a truly humane society in which animals are respected for their intrinsic value, and where the human-animal bond is strong.

Want to help animals? We have plenty of suggestions. Adopt a pet from a local shelter, join The Humane Society and be a part of our work to help companion animals and wildlife. You will be funding our educational, legislative, investigative and outreach projects in the U.S. and across the globe.

Or perhaps you'd like to make a memorial donation in honor of a pet, friend or relative? You can through our Kindred Spirits program. And if you'd like to contribute in a more structured way, our Planned Giving Office has suggestions about estate planning, annuities, and even gifts of stock that avoid capital gains taxes.

Maybe you have land that you would like to preserve as a lasting habitat for wildlife. Our Wildlife Land Trust can help you. Perhaps the land you want to share is a backyard— that's enough. Our Urban Wildlife Sanctuary Program will show you how to create a habitat for your wild neighbors.

So you see, it's easy to help animals. And The HSUS is here to help.

THE HUMANE SOCIETY
OF THE UNITED STATES.

2100 L Street NW • Washington, DC 20037 • 202-452-1100

www.hsus.org

AUTHOR DEDICATION & BIOGRAPHY

First, to my husband David, who wrestled babies, folded laundry and washed dishes so I could have more work time. To Alex for keeping his little brother entertained and being understanding when dinner was late. To Danny, who reminded me when it was time to turn off the computer.

To Kelly, for her support and encouragement. No one should have to put up with having me for a little sister. Sorry about that makeup incident.

To Kammi and Brian for coming through for me when it was crunch time.

Finally, to Scott for teaching me what magic words could hold.

Janet Engle has over ten years of experience working in the retail industry. Along with operating her own online specialty store, **www.oddmountain.com**, she helps other businesses create marketing materials and strategies.

Janet's first novel, <u>The Synergy of Avintia</u>, was published in 2002. She has also written numerous nonfiction articles about advertising, technology, and time management for business owners.

As the editor of the <u>International Data Rescue News</u>, Janet works with scientists and activists across the world to save historical environmental records. For more information about data rescue, please visit **www.iedro.org**.

CONTENTS

FOREWORD

By Dan Butler

The retail environment today is more competitive than ever, and the dynamic evolution of specialty retailing, the resurgence of department store retailing, and the continual growth of the online e-tailing makes this one of the most exciting times to be engaged in the retail environment. How to Open and Operate a Financially Successful Retail Business shares great insights into the many different aspects of retailing in a straightforward and well-organized approach that speaks to the diverse demands of retailing in today's economy. Like the National Retail Federation (NRF), this book covers a broad range of topics, all of which are important to a retail business owner.

The NRF is the world's largest and most influential retail trade association, working to provide thought leadership throughout the retail industry. The NRF encourages you to use this book to help further your understanding of retailing and to help guide you on your continued journey. It is our hope that your study of the retail industry reveals diversified challenges and opportunities for a fulfilling career that can last a lifetime. We encourage you to visit the NRF Web site at www.nrf.com. The NRF Pressroom and Bookstore are areas that may also assist you in your search for knowledge about the world of retailing.

Dan Butler joined NRF in December 2000. He is responsible for committee meetings of top retail executives, developing conference programming, and ensuring that NRF members are well-informed on the cutting-edge of retail industry issues. Butler serves as the NRF liaison to several member committees, including the Human Resources Executives Council and Council on Diversity. He also coordinates the yearly retail HR Executives Summit.

Butler is a retail veteran with over 26 years of store-line experience in retail management, merchandising, and human resources. His career includes a history of exceeding sales plans, reducing associate turnover, and achieving inventory control objectives.

Prior to joining NRF, Butler was Vice President and Store Manager at Macy's department store in Miami, Florida. While at Macy's he managed a store with $48 million in annual sales volume and successfully reduced both internal and external shrinkage. Before joining Macy's in 1998, Butler spent 11 years with

Hecht's department stores, first as divisional sales manager and then as store manager for stores in central Pennsylvania. He was named Divisional Sales Manager of the Year twice while at Hecht's.

Daniel Butler

Vice President Retail Operations

National Retail Federation

THE HISTORY OF RETAILING

The beginning of the retail industry is intimately tied to the history of mankind. As communication between different clans developed, trade was one of the first orders of business. This farmer had a surplus of wheat, that one had extra wool. Both would benefit through an exchange of goods.

The early marketplace became more efficient with the development of money. Early producers no longer had to find the right chain of people to exchange goods with – they could just sell their surplus then buy what they needed.

Primitive trade revolved around seasonal harvests, but eventually permanent shops were established. Producers began raising extra livestock, weaving more material than their family used, or growing surplus crops to sell at the market. The retail culture was born.

In the late 1600s, Hudson's Bay Company (HBC) established the world's first department store. HBC was also the first commercial corporation in North America. Dealing mainly in furs, tools, and hunting equipment, HBC was a far cry from the department stores of today.

As villages and towns sprung up across the United States and Canada, "general stores" followed. General stores allowed settlers to trade their furs, vegetables, game, and handcrafts in exchange for essentials such as flour, sugar, and salt. In addition, most stores carried cloth, tools, candy, and even ready-made clothing. The general store was often the center of commerce for a rural community.

In 1785, Gostiny Dvor opened its doors in St. Petersburg, Russia. Consisting of over 100 individual shops gathered under one roof, it is often considered the world's first shopping mall.

By the late 19th century, department stores were popping up in all the large European cities: Le Bon Marché in Paris, Jenners in Edinburgh, Delany's New Mart in Dublin, and Clery's in London. This new breed of department store had a wider selection of household and personal goods than Hudson's Bay Company. Their merchandise was chosen to appeal to a more sophisticated, urban market.

The retail revolution was not lost on the New World. In New York, the uptown shopping district was home to Macy's, Lord and Taylor, McCreary's, and Abraham & Straus. By 1900, Philadelphia had Wannamaker's and Salt Lake City was home to Zion's Cooperative Mercantile Institution. The corporate predecessor of Target, Dayton's Daylight, opened in Minneapolis in 1902.

During this time, specialty stores remained major players in the retail world. Although hats, books, electronics, and musical instruments were sold in large department stores, smaller niche stores maintained their clientele by offering a wider selection of merchandise and better customer service. As small towns saw their populations grow throughout the 20th century, the local general stores grew too. Many grew into independent department stores or were bought by larger chains.

The 1950s saw the rise of the discount department store, which offered clothing, household goods, and jewelry at significantly lower prices. These discount department stores usually lacked the grand architectural styling and name brand merchandise found at traditional department stores, opting instead for warehouse-like retail spaces and products that could be priced to appeal to more budget-conscious customers.

With the success of discount department store chains such as Wal-Mart, Target, and Kmart, retailers began to use the "big box" discount model to sell other types of goods, such as home and office supplies and electronics.

Although a few large chains seem to dominate the retail landscape, there is plenty of room for the small, independent store. Small retail businesses can offer specialty merchandise or services that large chains ignore. With the growing acceptance of internet-based stores, entrepreneurs can start their retail business from their own home and run it in their spare time.

TYPES OF RETAIL BUSINESSES

One of the first and most important decisions to make about a fledgling retail business is the format. Should a variety of merchandise from many wholesalers be chosen and sold from a storefront, or is selling from a Web site preferred? Should a franchise be bought or should a sales network be built?

Before committing to a business, it is imperative to understand the different formats and decide which is best.

TRADITIONAL

A "traditional" retail business sells merchandise through a physical store. Whether located downtown, at a mall, or as a stand-alone building outside of town, traditional retail businesses allow customers to browse and purchase merchandise. Traditional retailers may have contracts — even exclusive deals — with wholesalers, but after a contract expires, the store owners are usually free to make deals with any suppliers.

Owning a traditional retail business offers a high degree of independence and flexibility. The owner decides when the store is open and what is sold. However, for some business owners this freedom can be overwhelming. While it may be fun to put together lines and design displays, return policies and advertising campaigns must also be established. A traditional retailer may have to compete with retail chains that have more purchasing power and professionals constantly working on marketing strategies.

FRANCHISES

Franchises are becoming increasingly popular, with the same retail stores found in cities and towns throughout the country.

When buying a franchise, the rights to use trademarks and business methods are purchased. Franchisees usually pay monthly or quarterly franchise royalties, which are often a percentage of gross profits.

Because franchise companies want to maintain a certain business image and quality, they usually require franchisees to run their businesses a specific way. The franchise company may have strict rules about what hours a franchise must be open, what merchandise can be offered and for what price, how employees dress, and how financial records are kept. Failure to follow the rules may cause the franchise agreement to be cancelled.

Owning a franchise usually means less independence for the business owner, but it does have some advantages. Franchise companies usually run professionally-designed advertisements that benefit all their franchisees. They often offer specialized training for business owners, as well as advice about choosing a location. A franchise agreement often includes the guarantee that the company will not grant another franchise within a certain radius.

By buying a franchise, a business that already has an image and a reputation is being acquired, meaning much of the work is already done. However, if the national image of the franchise is tarnished, the damage may be seen in individual stores' bottom lines.

ONLINE/MAIL ORDER

Like a traditional retail establishment, an online or catalog store allows the owner to choose the merchandise, pricing, and marketing strategies. However, in a pure online or mail order business the store is "virtual" – customers browse the internet or print catalog and place their orders by e-mail, mail, or telephone.

One of the major advantages of this format is the low overhead and startup costs. Unless extra space is needed to store inventory, there will be no rent, utilities, or display costs. Many small retail businesses started as purely mail order or internet shops.

Running an online or mail order store may allow the owner to hold another job while building the business. This can take the pressure off to turn a profit right away, and may allow for some extra funds.

The line between traditional retail stores and online shops has become blurred in recent years, and many businesses find it beneficial to have both a brick-and-mortar and Internet presence.

DIRECT SALES/NETWORK MARKETING

Direct sales, also called *multilevel marketing* (MLM) or *network marketing*, is another type of retail business. The term "private franchise" is sometimes used to refer to a direct sales opportunity. Everything from cookware to food is sold by direct sales companies.

In direct sales, products specified by the parent company are sold and other people are recruited to join the sales team. A percentage of sales made can be earned, as well as a percentage from all the sales of recruits.

MLM businesses usually have comparatively low overhead and startup costs. Like franchises, MLM parent companies offer training and motivational tools. There are often very strict rules about how to market the business.

Unlike franchises, MLMs generally do not offer territory protection. Sometimes the company will stress recruitment over retail sales. Securing a business loan for a network marketing company is often difficult.

WHICH IS BEST FOR YOU?

The best format depends largely on a person's strengths, lifestyle, and how much time, money, and energy can be invested in the venture.

If a venture that can be done in one's spare time or while holding down another job is sought, an online or direct sales business may be a good fit. Individualists who will not be happy without complete autonomy over all business decisions should consider a traditional shop. For professional guidance, consider a franchise.

Do not feel pigeonholed by personal finances when deciding on the business format that will offer the best chance of success. Even if personal funds are limited, the money for a worthwhile business venture using other sources may be raised.

CASE STUDY: NETWORK MARKETING

Through his Web site **www.tribble.org**, Ty Tribble helps companies and individuals involved with direct sales take advantage of internet marketing techniques. He also retails Univera LifeSciences biotech and natural health products at **tribblet.agelesslife.com**.

"Most people make network marketing too complicated," Ty says. "If you sell *some* products and sponsor *some* people, you will make *some* money in network marketing. If you sell *a lot* of products and sponsor *a lot* of people, you will make *a lot* of money. The reality of network marketing is that most people do not sell products or sponsor people. They get involved with a business in the network marketing industry, and then they fail to network or market."

Ty recommends that entrepreneurs considering starting an MLM company find one that sells a unique, preferably patented product.

"The product should be something that you would be willing to tell others about, even if you were not involved with the company," Ty advises.

Corporate and field leadership are other important considerations, along with the company's compensation plan.

Ty stresses the importance of thoroughly researching a company's history before becoming involved.

"There are two times in the life of a network marketing company that you do not want to be involved in. The first is the *ground floor*. A high number of new companies do not make it past five years in this industry. Be careful with brand new companies. The second period to avoid is the *ceiling*. Companies that are not showing double digit growth will be much more difficult to build. Find out the real growth numbers by calling the company. The biggest companies are not always the best in terms of payout, reputation, and growth, but you do want to find a company that is stable. Take your time and do a lot of research."

According to Ty, nothing can take the place of passion and enthusiasm for the product.

"Want to be a success in network marketing? Find a product that you really love and tell other people about it."

3

WHAT TO EXPECT AS A BUSINESS OWNER

BENEFITS OF OWNING A RETAIL BUSINESS

Retail businesses have been the cornerstone of commerce throughout history. People open stores for a variety of reasons. Some of the benefits retail business owners enjoy include:

- **Constant challenges:** Owning a retail business will provide ample opportunity to master new skills for those who yearn to learn and grow. There will always be new ways of marketing the business, new paths for merchandising and branding, and new chances to improve customer and employee relations. A retail business never has to grow stagnant. As industry technology and consumer tastes change, a business can stay on top of trends and grow as large as desired.

- **No income limit:** For the retail business owner, there is no limit to the amount of profit that can be generated. A sound, well-researched plan, hard work, and creativity can yield a generous income. Of course, there are no guarantees. Even great ideas sometimes do not pan out.

- **Flexibility:** The owner of a business can tweak the operating hours to benefit his or her lifestyle. This is especially true of online or mail-order businesses. Flexibility might be more limited for a traditional brick-and-mortar store, but an hour can certainly be scheduled, especially during slow periods, to take care of personal tasks.

- **Respect:** Many people want to own a business, but very few do. As someone who has taken the plunge, a business owner might be in a position of authority within the community. By becoming involved in the Chamber of Commerce or other professional organizations, a position as a business leader can be taken.

- **Power:** Retail store owners have the power to take advantage of wholesale prices and bring exclusive merchandise to patrons. Offering a unique, in-demand inventory is good for business.

- **Personal satisfaction:** If a business owner enjoys what he or she is doing, then the long hours required to make a retail business successful will go quicker.

DISADVANTAGES OF OWNING A RETAIL BUSINESS

After reading the previous list, owning a retail business might seem ideal. Who in their right mind would pass up an endeavor that provides flexibility, big money, respect, power, and personal satisfaction?

Many retail business owners find that their professional life is not as easy as they thought. Some of the disadvantages of owning a retail business include:

- **Having many little bosses:** Employees answer to only one or two superiors, but a retail business owner must strive to please every single person that walks through the door. If a certain level of customer service is not provided, it will hurt the bottom line.

- **There is financial risk:** Nothing is guaranteed when owning a retail business. A steady paycheck cannot be counted on. Even if the store is doing brisk business, that can end abruptly. Even inventory may alter if a supplier goes out of business. Good employees can quit. Customers' tastes change. A "big box store" may open up next door, offering similar merchandise at lower prices. Owning a retail business can end up costing a good bit of money. Fortunately, this risk can be reduced by doing research and approaching a business responsibly. However, no business venture is a sure thing.

- **Feeling stressed:** As a business owner, it may be hard to leave professional worries at work. Owners may obsess about the big and little management details even during off hours.

- **Taking it personally:** It is difficult not to feel responsible if a customer has an unsatisfactory experience. Some people internalize every problem and see it as a reflection on their competence.

- **Losing career momentum:** If the owner decides to close his or her store and go back to a job, he or she may only be offered a lower position than if time away from the career track had not been taken to pursue business ambitions.

MISCONCEPTIONS ABOUT BUSINESS OWNERSHIP

- **Getting to set the hours:** One of the most common reasons people want to own their own business is for flexibility. Those who picture taking a summer day off to stroll along the beach or closing shop early on a Saturday to go to a child's tee-ball game may be disappointed. Business owners can certainly set the store's hours. Flexibility is an advantage of owning a retail shop. However, if too many customers are disappointed, business might not be booming for long. Buyers will want to visit a store on their schedule, not on the owner's.

- **There are big tax breaks for businesses:** Many people have heard that there are many tax breaks related to owning a business. Unfortunately, most of these tax breaks require a business to lose money first. While an accountant can help maximize the tax benefits related to the retail business, owners may be surprised at how much profit will end up going to the government.

- **Making money:** Many businesses struggle to break even, let alone make a profit.

- **To be successful, jumping in with both feet is necessary:** It is possible to run a retail store, especially one that is online-based, and not give up a day job. This gives an owner the benefit of a regular paycheck while the business grows.

THE "AVERAGE" DAY

Most retail business owners wear many hats throughout the typical day. Even when not on the sales floor, the owner has to know enough about sales to make sure employees are doing their jobs. Even if a bookkeeper or accountant is hired, the owner still needs to be knowledgeable enough about the company's finances to make sure the records look reasonable. A business might use a graphic artist to design ads, but the owner is the one in charge of the long-term and short-term marketing plans.

On any given day, a business owner might deal with suppliers, customers, employees, and contractors. The owner might have to handle repairs to the store and research product lines. One day might call for an owner to be dressed in a suit and meeting with bankers, while the next might call for old overalls while painting the shop walls.

There is no such thing as an "average" day in retail sales. Each day presents different challenges and the opportunity to learn, adjust, and improve the business.

CASE STUDY: DRAGON WHISPERS HARP SUPPLIES

Betty Roan Truitt started Dragon Whispers Harp Supplies (**www. dragonwhispers.com**) in 1980, after a two year apprenticeship with another harp company. During her apprenticeship, she discovered that there was an untapped market for specialty harp equipment such as levers, sounding boards, and tuning pins.

Wearing different hats and not being afraid to tackle any task is integral to small business success, according to Betty.

"Be prepared to do everything — sweep your own floors, design your own ads, and find your own sales niche. Be prepared to have enough wherewithal to provide for you and your family for at least three years, as it will take that and perhaps more time to gain recognition."

Retailing to a limited market is difficult, but the rewards can be great.

"Having your own business is the best of all possible worlds, but is very hard work," says Betty. "There is no 40-hour week; it is more like 60 to 80 hours. You need to be a self-starter. At times this is difficult, but if you love what you are doing, it really is not a hardship."

4

SKILLS FOR SUCCESS

Not everyone is cut out to own a retail business. Taking a careful inventory of skills and personality traits before investing in a store may save time, money, and heartache.

ORGANIZATION

A business owner will have to wear many different hats. Basic bookkeeping must be understood, even if an accountant is hired. Being able to analyze the success of advertising campaigns is essential, even if a marketing consultant is used. The owner needs to be a salesperson, buyer, boss, and visionary.

When the business starts rolling, the amount of paperwork generated may be a shock. An organizational system should be established for the receipts, invoices, orders, withholding forms, and paychecks. Appointments and due dates will have to be managed. Missing appointments can result in waiting several weeks for another appointment.

To be an effective store owner, organize projects, paperwork, ideas, and time. There are computer programs that can help with the tasks, but the bottom line is that the owner will need to make the effort to use the software. A disorganized person may become easily overwhelmed.

LEADERSHIP

All decisions end with the business owner. If an interior decorator is hired to create a look for the retail space, the owner will be to blame if the fixtures do not match the store's image. If an employee is rude to a customer, the owner will be held accountable because he or she is the one that sets the policies.

This may sound unfair, but leadership is an important aspect of business ownership. In the end, owners make the decisions then deal with the fallout — both good and bad.

People that blame others when things do not go right or that do not like to give direction and instigate change may find that owning a store is not as much fun as originally thought.

PERSONALITY

The heart of owning a store is making sales. Owners will need to offer people what they want, or convince them that they need to have what is being sold.

An owner will need to be a *people person*. Those who are outgoing and comfortable making small talk with anyone who may enter the door may find that their personality is just right for the retail world. Those who are full of complaints about suppliers, employees, profits, and life in general will make customers uncomfortable — which is not good for repeat business.

FLEXIBILITY

Very little in the retail world is the same as it was just ten years ago. New technology has made it easier to buy goods online. Large discount chains are opening stores in small towns everywhere. Successful businesses are those that can change with the times. If a competitor moves in across the street, an owner will need to be flexible enough to carve out a niche and differentiate his or her business. If some of the core inventory becomes unavailable, a new focus for the store might be needed.

Those who are become attached to routines and fight change because "that is not the way we have always done it" may find it difficult to overcome new challenges.

CREATIVITY

Owning a store allows a person to be a sort of artist. The way the retail space is laid out, displays are designed, and windows are decorated can all help the bottom line. Fortunately, those who are not creative by nature can follow some principles that will help in crafting attractive designs.

PERSEVERANCE

One of the most important qualities a retail shop owner needs to have is perseverance. Most businesses will have seasonal swings. Successful owners do not give up the store at the first sales slow down. They use business cycles to tweak their policies, prepare for high sales periods, learn new skills, plan marketing campaigns, or network within the industry.

Those who lack the ability to stick to a project for very long or are bored easily may find that owning a retail business is not a good fit. Even when sales are slow, successful retail owners tend to find things they can do to improve their business.

EVALUATING YOUR SKILLS

The following worksheet can help a person gauge his or her strengths and weaknesses as a potential retail business owner.

SKILLS FOR SUCCESS		
Read the descriptions and circle which best describes you		
Organization		
My workspace always seems to be cluttered. Where do all those papers come from?	1 2 3 4 5	I can always find paperwork. After I use something, I always return it to where it belongs.
Leadership		
I would rather someone else call the shots. No one listens to my input, anyway.	1 2 3 4 5	I find it easy to take charge of a situation. People respect me and enjoy following my lead.

SKILLS FOR SUCCESS		
Personality		
I tend to rub people the wrong way.	1 2 3 4 5	I can get along with anyone. I am definitely a "people person."
Flexibility		
If it is not on the schedule, it makes me nervous.	1 2 3 4 5	I can roll with the punches. I can handle any problem without breaking a sweat.
Creativity		
I would rather follow a checklist than have to devise a solution from scratch.	1 2 3 4 5	My head is always racing with ideas. I am always looking for a new or better way of getting the job done.
Perseverance		
If it does not come easy, it is not worth doing.	1 2 3 4 5	I always see tasks through to completion, no matter what.

After an honest skills evaluation, those who find they are lacking in one or more of the above qualities should consider what can be done to improve the "problem areas." Can a class in organization and time management be taken? Volunteer for a leadership role for a local fundraising event? Take a part-time job in a busy, changing environment to learn to be more flexible?

5

EXPERIMENTING WITH RETAIL SALES

Being a business owner can bring many benefits, but it is not the lifestyle for everyone. The hours can be long, working with customers and employees can be frustrating, and the market is constantly changing.

For those who are unsure if owning a retail store is right for them, consider "trying out" the experience before investing too much time and energy. There are many ways to test the waters of retail sales before diving in headfirst.

WORKING IN A RETAIL ESTABLISHMENT

One of the quickest and easiest ways to see if owning and operating a store will be enjoyable is to work at someone else's shop. Store employees have the chance to learn how to close a sale, operate a cash register, and deal with unsatisfied customers. By gaining experience with store policies, potential store owners will be able to see first hand what works and what needs improvement.

Many shop managers and owners are pleased when employees take an interest in more than what time their shift ends. They can be wonderful resources for learning about suppliers, marketing, and financing.

Use the opportunity of working at a retail business to learn as much as possible about the retail world. Keep notes about which policies should be copied and which ones undermine employee morale. Which managerial traits are effective in motivating employees? What makes a good retail employee? What should be done differently?

RUNNING AN ONLINE AUCTION STORE

Establishing a shop at an online auction site is another way of gaining retail experience. Start by cleaning out the closet and auctioning the clutter. Be sure to keep accurate records about shipping, fees and profits.

Many things about the retail world can be learned from online auctions. Experiment with the auctions and learn what kind of merchandise sells, what wording pulls in potential bidders, and how to maximize customer satisfaction.

To gain even more experience, look into buying products wholesale, creating items, or buying collectibles at yard sales and auctioning them online.

TEMPORARY RETAIL BOOTHS

For those who believe they already have a desirable product, setting up a table at a craft show, farmer's market, or bazaar can help them learn about many business and marketing principles.

Temporary retail events offer the chance to experiment with how to best display products and what price points yield the most sales. These events present the opportunity to practice customer service and to evaluate good and bad vendors. The local show circuit can be a great way to learn about record keeping and to see what kind of clientele is attracted to the product.

Because they are usually held on weekends and often have low vendor fees, fairs and shows can provide an extensive retail education.

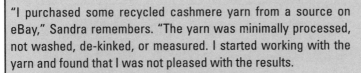

The Internet is the source of many opportunities for entrepreneurs. For Sandra Hudecek, owner of White Tail Acres Yarns and Things, the auction site eBay was the inspiration for her business.

"I purchased some recycled cashmere yarn from a source on eBay," Sandra remembers. "The yarn was minimally processed, not washed, de-kinked, or measured. I started working with the yarn and found that I was not pleased with the results.

"The kinks in the yarn made my knitting look awful, so I wound the yarn into skeins and washed it hoping to remove the kinks. Washing the yarn did not remove the kinks, but much to my amazement, my pretty peach yarn actually turned out to be a lovely light pink color when all the dirt was washed out. At this point I was relatively unimpressed with my yarn purchase, and I knew I could do much better."

Now Sandra sells recycled yarn, especially cashmere, through her own eBay store.

For Sandra, owning a successful business means being dedicated.

"You can not run a successful business if you are not willing to meet your commitments. Owning a business is work. It is not always going to be fun or exciting. You have to get up and out of bed, go to work, and meet the commitments you have obligated yourself to meet even when you do not feel like it."

6

ORGANIZING YOUR BUSINESS

The question of how to organize a business arises early in the startup process. The structure of a retail business has legal, tax, and liability implications. It will determine what paperwork needs to be filed with the state and local authorities, and influence what accounting software is chosen.

Although a legal organization must be decided on before officially starting the business, the choice may be changed. Many businesses modify structure as they grow.

The three basic choices for legal organizations are sole proprietorships, partnerships, and corporations.

SOLE PROPRIETORSHIPS

The *sole proprietorship* is the default business structure. Unless a business declares otherwise, the government considers it a sole proprietorship. The owner is the *sole proprietor*.

In terms of paperwork, a sole proprietorship is the quickest and cheapest form of business to start. It is also the easiest structure to dissolve. For many people who choose this organization, the major benefit is the independence — the owner gets to make all the decisions and gets to keep any profit.

This independence also brings some disadvantages. The sole owner of the company is held responsible for any business liability. If a customer is hurt in the store and the owner is found liable, the owner is responsible for any difference between the cost of the accident and what the insurance pays.

Personal assets are connected to the business, and a person's credit rating can be affected by the business's performance. In a sole proprietorship, any accounts, loans, or lines of credit in the "business's name" are really in the owner's name. Late payments can lower a personal credit score. If a debt is run up and then the business is closed, the owner remains responsible for paying the balance.

Remember, unless legally declared otherwise, a business is a sole proprietorship.

PARTNERSHIPS

Unlike a sole proprietorship, in a *partnership* the company is owned by two, three, or more people.

A partnership is only marginally more difficult to form than a sole proprietorship. Usually there is a verbal or written agreement between the parties, establishing how much input and how much profit each partner will share. Beyond that, forming a partnership in most places requires simply putting all partners' names on leases, contracts, and other business documents related to the company.

There are many reasons people form partnerships. Spreading the costs of ownership among more than one person may be the only way to finance the business. Sometimes partners are able to compensate for each others' weaknesses. If one person is a good organizer and financial planner, for instance, and the other is a remarkable salesperson, creating a partnership may give the business its best chance of success.

Like a sole proprietorship, the personal finances of the owners are linked to the company. Owners may be responsible for the business's liabilities and credit problems.

Unfortunately, partnerships can be breeding grounds for conflict. Whenever more than one person is a decision maker, there can be disagreement. Partners may squabble over what direction to guide the business in or what percentage of the profits to reinvest in the company. One partner might think the other is not working hard enough at the business, or want to dissolve the business while the other does not.

One way to minimize the potential for problems is to create a detailed partnership agreement and have it reviewed by an attorney. The agreement should include:

- The percentage of any profits that will go to each partner.

- The percentage of any losses that each partner is responsible for.

- The specific business duties of each partner.

- How the financial records of the business will be kept and who will have access to them.

- What happens to any business assets if the partnership is dissolved.

- What happens to the business if a partner dies.

- How decisions will be made if there is conflict.

The following sample partnership agreement is also found on the accompanying CD.

SAMPLE PARTNERSHIP AGREEMENT

Date of agreement: June 28, 2006

Parties of agreement (Partner's Names):

Katherine Sawyer

Raymond Greer

Business name: Coalfield Gifts

SAMPLE PARTNERSHIP AGREEMENT

Main product/service of business: Crafts produced by Appalachian artisans

Business Address:

817 East Fourth Street

Beckley, West Virginia

The partnership will begin on : June 28, 2006

The partnership will continue until: Until Terminated

Profits and Losses: The net profits and losses will be divided equally between the partners.

Specific Duties: The partners will each devote at least 40 hours per week to the business. The partners will have equal rights to the business. Neither partner will make management or monetary decisions (including borrowing or lending money, signing an agreement, or purchasing or selling property) regarding the business without he consent of the other partner.

Financial Records: The business's financial records will be kept at the business's main office. Both partners will have full access to the books. The books will be closed and balanced at the end of the fiscal year.

Death: If either partner should die during the course of the partnership, the surviving partner will have the right to purchase the interest from the estate of the deceased or to terminate and liquidate the business. The surviving partner will have 30 days from the death of the deceased partner to inform, in writing, the estate of the deceased.

Dissolution: The partnership can be terminated at any time by the agreement of the partners. Upon dissolution, the business will be liquidated. After paying any business liabilities, the net from the liquidation will be divided equally between the partners.

Disagreements: Any disagreements regarding the partnership will be settled by a mutually agreed on arbitrator.

Signature of partner:

_____

Signature of partner:

_____

Date: _____

Partnerships do not have to be 50-50. One owner may be content to be a financial resource and let the other make all business decisions. One partner may work at the business full time, while the other puts in a half-day once a week. There is no "right way" to form a partnership. Remember that however it is structured, all partners need to understand the arrangement and be in agreement.

CORPORATIONS

A corporation is different from a sole proprietorship or partnership in that it is separate from the owners. The owners are not personally responsible for the corporation's liabilities.

Forming a corporation involves more paperwork than a sole proprietorship or partnership. The process can be expensive and confusing. With a corporation, the business's earnings cannot simply be used at will; any profits must be issued as a dividend to stockholders.

There are several types of corporations, including subchapter S corporations and limited liability corporations (LLC), which differ in how profits and losses are taxed. An accountant can help determine which type of corporation is best for a business.

CASE STUDY: SOUTH PAW STUDIOS — KATY MIMS DESIGNS

Katy Mims has sold her handcrafted beaded and wire wrapped jewelry since 1997, but she officially started South Paw Studio — Katy Mims Designs in 2001.

"I design and make all my jewelry," explains Katy. "I do not use prefabricated kits or patterns. I am not a reseller of imported or manufactured jewelry. I feel that needs to be stated since in the past two or three years, the beading industry has been making it easier and easier for people to make their own beaded jewelry with no artistic skill involved.

"I sell my necklaces, bracelets, earrings, rings, and crystal bookmarks. My primary customers are women. Of course, there are some men that are interested in my jewelry. I attract all age ranges. I do some contemporary pieces that are appealing to the younger generation and I do some more elegant pieces that are longer in length and have more pearls. Those pieces appeal to the business suit wearing "Baby Boomer" crowd.

CASE STUDY: SOUTH PAW STUDIOS — KATY MIMS DESIGNS

"I market to those two kinds of clients by selling in high-end galleries. I also create one-of-a-kind pieces for brides and bridal parties. Offering custom bridal sets is a great business since brides usually wants something that no one else has ever seen. I market to brides by setting up a display at a custom invitation shop. I show some prototypes and give them a little packet that includes a nice postcard with all my information and all the colors in which the Swarovski crystals are available.

"I tell them to contact me for a personal appointment where I can come to their home. Usually it is a fun event including the maid of honor and the mother of the bride. We mull over the look she wants for her girls, and we talk design and colors. It is now a part of the planning process for a wedding along with wedding invitations and flowers.

"If I had the first year of my business to do over again, I would have started as an LLC instead of a sole proprietorship. That way I could have had my own business line of credit without having to worry about stretching my family's financial limits.

"I also wish I would not have spent so much money on bad inventory. I bought some bad quality beads in the beginning and was busying them about once a week, which was not a good spending habit since I was paying a lot in shipping costs each month. Plus, with the beads being poor in quality, the work that I created did not sell as fast.

"Now, I choose my suppliers very carefully. They have to offer a good quality product at wholesale prices, with low shipping, and a quick turn around time. I do not want to wait five days for them to ship out my inventory. I usually want it shipped the same day or next day. I try to stay with companies that are on the east coast, since I can go with UPS ground and get the orders in two days. That saves on money.

"I also travel to private trade shows three times a year. I avoid shipping costs altogether and get to handpick my beads so I am not getting cracked, chipped, or half-drilled beads like I did in the beginning. Plus, when you are face-to-face with your dealer, they remember you. IF you are nice to them, they give you loyalty discounts on top of their show specials."

For more information about South Paw Studios — Katy Mims Designs, e-mail Southpawstudios@hotmail.com or visit **www.southpawonline.com.**

7

BUYING AN EXISTING STORE

Starting a retail store from scratch can be daunting. Purchasing an existing business can streamline the process, but it does have risks.

BENEFITS OF BUYING AN EXISTING STORE

There are many reasons entrepreneurs opt to purchase a store rather than start a new one:

- **Proven track record** — An existing business will likely come with a trail of paperwork, which can be used to analyze what sales techniques work and what should be changed.

- **Less startup effort** — When an existing store is purchased, it will usually come with some inventory, fixtures, and clientele.

- **Easier borrowing** — Many lenders prefer to finance an existing store that has shown a profit.

- **Increased chance of success** — Statistics suggest that about 80 percent of new businesses fail. For established businesses under new ownership, that number is closer to 20 percent.

- **Established relationships** — Odds are the current owners already have contracts and negotiated prices with certain vendors. They may have trademark or licensing agreements in place.

- **Knowledgeable staff** — A staff that is welcoming and helpful after the ownership transition can help the new owner understand how the business works, and see ways to make it improve.

DISADVANTAGES TO BUYING AN EXISTING STORE

Of course there is a downside to buying a business. Even those who think they know exactly what they are getting may find themselves dealing with some of these common problems:

- **Reputation** — When an existing business is bought, its reputation with the community is also being purchased. This can be a good thing, if the image of the store is one of quality merchandise and good customer service. However, customers who have had bad experiences with the business will not care if the store has been sold to new owners. They may not give the new ownership a chance to change their impressions.

- **Existing problems** — After a business is purchased, its problems become the new owner's. Even if a store has been showing a healthy profit that might only be because they have been scrimping on routine maintenance or updates. Extensive repairs for neglected or abused property, vehicles, or equipment may need to be invested in.

- **Hurt feelings** — Employees or suppliers that feel betrayed by the sale can be destructive to the business's property, reputation, and image.

- **More difficult to change** — With a store room full of merchandise, a new owner may find that it is not cost effective to change the focus of the store. Even a name change can be very expensive when the cost of new signs, stationery, and marketing material is factored in. A new owner may find himself or herself stuck in a business that is not understood or enjoyed.

USING A BUSINESS BROKER

When considering purchasing a business, do not limit the search to the choices listed in the local classified ads. A business broker may know owners that are thinking about selling, but do not want to advertise. A broker can also help the search branch out to include industries and locations that had not been considered. In addition, a broker may have connections with potential loan institutions or business partners.

Most states have a *Business Brokers Association* that can help when choosing a qualified broker. In most situations, the business broker makes money when the transaction is complete. The broker will try to show each business in the best possible light. Be sure to research the facts about any store before agreeing to purchase it.

Buying a business can be a major financial investment. An attorney will likely be needed to negotiate the contract, and an accountant will help with the finer points of the financial statements. Be leery if a broker claims that independent advisors are not needed.

ANALYZING THE LOCATION

Location will influence a business's chances of success in the long-term and in the short-term. A store on a remote street outside of town may be a good buy, especially if the city is growing and an increase in traffic near the business is expected. On the other hand, a store on a busy street corner may be doomed if it is in a town with a rapidly decreasing population.

Researching the location of the store is an important step toward determining if the business will be a good investment. After studying traffic patterns and demographic trends, it might be decided that the business does not have much potential for future growth. If the decision to make an offer is reached, understanding more about the location can lead to more power when negotiating a sales price.

The following are important details to consider about the store's location:

- **Local trends** — How is the area changing? Is the population increasing? What is the age profile of the residents?

- **Traffic** — How many people pass the store everyday? Are there any construction plans that will change the traffic patterns around the store?

- **Competition** — Are there other stores offering the same merchandise nearby? Having competition is not necessarily a deal breaker, but have a plan in mind to differentiate the business.

- **Visibility** — Do people know the store is there? Are there adequate signs?

- **Accessibility** — Can people get to the store easily? Is there parking? Have considerations been made for those with limited mobility?

- **Convenience** — Will the owner be able to commute to the store easily?

- **Image** — Does the image of the location fit what customers want? If the products will be marketed toward an upscale crowd, a location in a low rent area might turn customers away. When trying to attract a bohemian, free-spirited clientele, a storefront in the center of the corporate district may not be optimal.

The following worksheet will help to determine if the location of an existing business is an asset or a liability.

LOCATION ANALYSIS		
Read the descriptions and circle the number which best describes the location		
Local Trends		
The local population is declining.	1 2 3 4 5	The location is having a population boom.
There are not many people in the area in the income bracket of my target market.	1 2 3 4 5	The average income for the area is the same as that of my target market.

LOCATION ANALYSIS		
There are not many people in the area in the age range of my target market.	1 2 3 4 5	The majority of the population is at or below the age of my target market.
Traffic		
The store is out of the way. Customers would have to make a special trip to get there.	1 2 3 4 5	Current traffic patterns take many people by the store.
Future construction will have traffic bypassing the store.	1 2 3 4 5	Future construction will bring more traffic by the store.
Competition		
There are several stores nearby that offer the same or similar merchandise.	1 2 3 4 5	This is the only store of its type in the area.
Visibility		
The store is not visible from the road.	1 2 3 4 5	The store is visible for several blocks.
There are no signs.	1 2 3 4 5	Signs are large, highly visible and do not need to be upgraded.
Accessibility		
The store is difficult to get to. You have to know where you are going.	1 2 3 4 5	The entrance of the store is clearly marked and easy to find.
The parking is inadequate and will need to be improved immediately.	1 2 3 4 5	There is plenty of parking, more than enough for employees and customers.
The store is not handicap accessible. There are stairs, steps, or narrow walkways that would make it impossible for a customer in a wheelchair.	1 2 3 4 5	The store is fully accessible. enabling equipment has been installed to make the parking lot, entrance, selling floor, and restrooms easily navigable for customers with a range of disabilities.
Convenience		
The store is a long distance from my home. Commuting will be difficult.	1 2 3 4 5	The store is close to home. I can go back and forth several times a day.
Services such as accounting, shipping, and printing are not available in the area.	1 2 3 4 5	The store is close to all services I will use regularly.

LOCATION ANALYSIS						
Image						
The location's image is substantially different from the image of the intended clientele.	1	2	3	4	5	The location's image is identical to that of the intended clientele.
I would be embarrassed to own a business in this area.	1	2	3	4	5	I would be proud to own a business in this area.
The outside of the store would not attract customers. It needs immediate improvement.	1	2	3	4	5	The outside of the store is attractive and matches the image of the business.

Traffic Counts

If the initial analysis of a business's location checks out, take the time to do quantitative traffic counts. Having these counts can give more evidence about the potential profitability of a business, help identify other markets that may be served, and provide background information to possible financiers.

There are two types of traffic counts to consider performing: automotive and pedestrian.

To perform an elementary automotive traffic count, simply count the number of cars that pass the entrance of the store. Be sure to be in a safe position that will not influence traffic flow. Depending on the amount of traffic, an assistant or two may be needed to monitor different lanes. A thumb counter, available at most office supply stores, can be very useful in busy traffic situations.

For the best results, take readings at several different times of day. At the very least, sample in the morning, afternoon, and evening. Record the results at five or 15 minute increments.

To get even more data, record other characteristics about the passing traffic, such as:

- What percentage stop at the store?

- How many have out-of-state tags?

- Which direction are the vehicles coming from?

- How many people are in the average car?

- How many are commercial, versus privately owned, vehicles?

These characteristics do not have to be studied at the same time. After obtaining some reliable total traffic counts, consider just sampling cars for the other statistics.

Unless the business being analyzed depends almost entirely on vehicular traffic, a pedestrian traffic count may also be beneficial. If the store is at a busy location, limit the count to the number of people that appear to be members of the major demographic groups of the target market. For example, count women who look like they are between 25 and 40 years old.

If the majority of the company's business comes from foot traffic, consider expanding the pedestrian traffic count to include:

- The number of people that enter the store.

- The age and gender breakdown of pedestrian traffic.

- The direction most pedestrians are coming from.

- Factors that influence pedestrian traffic, such as bus schedule, nearby businesses, and weather.

KNOW WHAT YOU ARE GETTING

Before buying an existing business, it is important to review the financial health of the company. Two important documents to examine are the *balance sheet* and the *profit and loss statement*. Be careful if a company refuses to share one of these records.

A profit and loss statement shows whether a business made money or lost money during a designated time period. This record takes into account the business's starting inventory, the cost of purchasing additional merchandise, how much revenue came in, and how much was spent on marketing, packaging, wages, and other general expenses. In the following example, the business made a profit of $98,947 during 2006.

A single profitable year does not make a store a good investment. Before agreeing to purchase a business, review its history of annual profit and loss statements.

SAMPLE PROFIT & LOSS STATEMENT CALLE MENSWEAR		
Starting Date: 1/01/06	Ending Date 12/31/06	
INCOME		
Income From Sales		907,908
b. Beginning Inventory	45,987	
c. Purchases (1/01/06)	259,770	
d. C.O.G. Available Sale (b+c)	305,757	
e. Ending Inventory (12/31/06)	58,112	
Cost of Good Sold (d-e)		247,645
Gross Profit on Sales (IFS - COGS)		660,263
Expenses		
f. Advertising/Marketing	98,332	
g. Freight	2,785	
h. Order Fulfillment	17,445	
i. Packaging	3,556	
j. Wages	112,864	
k. Travel	3,264	
l. Depreciation (Product Assets)	1,948	
m. Other Variable (not fixed) Expenses	629	
Total Variable Expenses (add f through m)		240,821
n. Insurance	9,657	
o. Salaries	90,267	
p. Licenses	1,344	

SAMPLE PROFIT & LOSS STATEMENT		
q. Rent	13,897	
r. Utilities	23,564	
s. Administrative Costs	45,110	
t. Depreciation (equipment)	4,210	
u. Other Fixed Expenses	2,789	
Total Fixed Expenses (add n through u)		190,838
Total Operating Expenses (TVE + TFE)		431,659
Net Operational Income (GPS - TOE)		228,604
aa. Interest Income	2,159	
bb. Interest Expense	684	
Net Profit Before Tax (NOI + aa - bb)		230,079
cc. Federal Taxes	92,032	
dd. State Taxes	34,500	
ee. Local Taxes	4,600	
Total Taxes (cc+dd+ee)		131,132
NET PROFIT/LOSS AFTER TAXES (NPBT-TT)		98,947

The balance sheet shows a snapshot of the finances of a company at a specific time. The balance sheet details the company's assets, liabilities, and net worth. The left hand side of a balance sheet, the "total assets," will always equal the right hand side, or the "total liabilities."

BALANCE SHEET FOR CROWTOPIA TROPHIES AND AWARDS AS OF 7/12/06			
ASSETS		LIABILITIES	
Current Assets		Current Liabilities	
Cash and Equivalents	856	Accounts Payable	422
Petty Cash	52	Accrued Liabilities	180
Receivables	196	Accrued Income Taxes	318
Inventory	1,256	Long-Term Debt, due within one year	1,200
Prepaid Expenses	465	Capital Lease Obligations, due within one year	
Other Assets	92		

BALANCE SHEET FOR CROWTOPIA TROPHIES AND AWARDS AS OF 7/12/06			
TOTAL CURRENT ASSETS	2,917	TOTAL CURRENT LIABILITIES	2,120
Property and Equipment			
Buildings, Improvements	25,600	Long Term Debt	3,500
Fixtures, Equipment	1,600	Long Term Capital Lease Obligations	
Transportation Equipment	3,200	Deferred Income Tax	
Total Property and Equipment, at cost	27,520	Other	
Less Depreciation	(1,570)		
NET PROPERTY AND EQUIPMENT	25,950		
Property under Capital Lease	0		
Less Amortization	0		
Net Property under Capital Lease	25,950	OWNER'S EQUITY	20,901
Goodwill			
Other Assets	570		
TOTAL ASSETS	26,521	TOTAL LIABILITIES	26,521

There are three particularly important things to look for on a balance sheet: the company's assets, its liabilities, and its net worth.

Assets

The company's assets are everything that could be converted into cash. This usually includes cash, inventory, investments, prepaid goods or services, accounts receivable, land, equipment, buildings, furniture, and vehicles.

Liabilities

Liabilities include anything that a business owes, such as business loans, mortgages, accounts payable, taxes payable, and payroll accrual.

Net Worth

A business's net worth is simply its assets minus its liabilities. The net worth may be broken down different ways depending on if the business is a sole proprietorship, partnership, or corporation.

Balance sheets can reveal quite a bit about the current manager's skills. After reviewing them, patterns might emerge or ideas may form that can improve the company's bottom line.

Where the balance sheet indicates a business's monetary position at one point in time, the profit and loss statement (income statement) gives a picture of the company's long-term financial health. Businesses should prepare profit and loss statements after each business month and fiscal year.

Looking at a series of these statements will provide valuable information about the viability of the business before it is purchased. The information can also help make budgeting decisions after the purchase. For example, the time period when marketing efforts were most effective by yielding the most profit can be tracked.

Profit and loss statements are prepared using the general ledger and balance sheet. It will reveal the net sales, the cost of the goods sold, the gross profit, expenses, net income, tax payments, and net profit for the business over the specified period of time.

Be wary about buying a business that does not run regular profit and loss statements, refuses to show their statements, or has gaps in their records. They may be trying to hide the business's finances or they may not have been reliable about record keeping.

An accountant can help review the retail store's books and help determine if it would be a good investment.

VALUING ASSETS AND SETTING A PRICE

The current owners may have an asking price for the business. This price is usually set high to leave room for negotiation. In order to purchase a business at a fair price, it is important to understand exactly what is included in the sale and what it is worth.

The following are some types of property that might be included when buying a retail business:

- Land
- Buildings
- Parking lots
- Inventory
- Fixtures
- Tax credits
- Licensing agreements

- Equipment
- Furniture
- Business name
- Vendor contracts
- Financial records
- Supplies

- Marketing mailing lists
- Customer database
- Building lease agreements
- Utility connections
- Equipment rental contracts
- Advertising agreements
- Franchise agreements

Never assume that the purchase price includes these items. It may seem obvious that by buying a business, the name or the current inventory is also being purchased. To the owner, however, it may be equally obvious that he is taking those assets to his new location across town. Ask and get the answer in writing before you buy.

There are several ways to put a reasonable price tag on an existing retail business. Often the simplest method is the "cost approach." After coming to an understanding of what is to be included in the deal, determine how much it would cost to purchase everything separately. Do not forget to factor in shipping, installation, taxes, and depreciation.

There are several conditions the buyer or the seller can suggest that can affect the selling price. Some of the factors that may be in the purchase contract include:

- **Non-compete agreement:** The seller agrees not to operate a competing business within a specified radius for an agreed on period of time.

- **Consulting service:** The seller agrees to act as a consultant for the new business owner.

- **Seller buy back:** The buyer gives the seller the opportunity to buy the business back within a certain time frame, or offers the seller the first chance to buy the business if the new owner decides to sell.

- **Existing accounts receivable:** Who will be responsible for collecting outstanding funds, and who will receive the money?

- **Possession:** When will the new owner be able to take possession of the property?

- **Employee contact:** How much access will the buyer have to employees before closing or taking possession of the property?

FINANCING THE PURCHASE

When buying an existing retail store, there are four main choices for financing. The business can be purchased outright, using existing funds. In some situations, the owner may offer to finance the transaction. The money may also be borrowed from a bank or family member.

Purchase Outright

If enough cash is available, buying the business outright is an option. Because they will not have the hassle of dealing with a bank, the current owners may offer a price break if this route is chosen.

If the transaction depletes the backup funds, the new business or personal finances may suffer from the lack of operating capital.

Owner Financed

Some sellers may offer an owner-financing option, where a down payment is given, and then regular payments are made over a specified period of time. One of the advantages of owner-financing is that they might be more flexible with the terms of the agreement than a bank, especially if a large down payment is offered.

However, buying a business "on time" from the current owner might reduce the new owner's ability to run his or her own company. The seller might decide that he should have some say in decision making until he is paid in full.

Bank Financed

One of the most common ways to finance the purchase of a retail business is through a bank or a credit union. In order to obtain a bank loan, a business plan, an appraisal of the business being purchased, and a survey of any property involved in the transaction will be needed.

The ability to obtain a bank loan will depend on the buyer's personal financial situation and credit history, the value and selling price of the business, the buyer's personal contribution to the purchase, and the bank's determination of the buyer's ability to make the business a success.

Family/Friend Financed

It may be tempting to finance a business purchase through a friend or family member — especially if they offer a better rate and more favorable terms than the bank. When going this route, make sure to get all the details in writing, the same as when financing through the seller or a bank. More importantly, follow the conditions laid out in the contract. Do not rely on the goodwill of the lender to allow for skipped payments if finances become tight — it can lead to bad feelings within the family or the end to a friendship.

Like an owner financed situation, a personal loan through a friend or family member may limit independence. The lender may feel that they are entitled to give out business advice, and that the owner is obligated to take it.

COMPLETING THE DEAL

After a selling price is agreed on and the necessary financing has been secured, closing the deal can take 30-60 days.

The following people may be present at closing:

- Buyer
- Seller
- Buyer's real estate agent
- Seller's real estate agent
- Business broker

- Buyer's attorney
- Seller's attorney
- Loan officer
- Family members

At closing, be certain to look over any papers that are signed and discuss any confusing details with an attorney. Refuse to be rushed or pressured to sign until the written terms of the agreement are fully understood.

At closing, the current owner will complete a *bill of sale*, which the buyer and a witness may also have to sign. An example bill of sale is below and also on the accompanying CD.

BILL OF SALE

The undersigned, Robert Pearl, hereby sells, transfers, and conveys to Daniel Carter all the properties, effects, and goods listed below, and the whole of the Tractor Direct business formerly owned and operated by the undersigned, and acknowledges receipt of sufficient consideration for the same.

The undersigned warrants that said properties and goods are clear of all encumbrances and that it has the right to sell the same.

The undersigned agrees not to operate a retail tractor and tractor parts business within 5 years of the date of this agreement within 25 miles of 123 Broad Street, Springfield, KY.

Seller Signature:_____
Date:

Seller Signature:_____
Date:

SMOOTHING THE TRANSITION

After a suitable retail business has been found, a fair price has been negotiated, and the deal has been, many people might be tempted to think that the hard work is over.

Do not be fooled into thinking that everything will be easier now that the transaction is complete. The business still must be guided through a successful transition of ownership.

Employees

Successfully communicating with the business's current employees is often a crucial step toward an easy transition. If the employees support the new owner, they can be a valuable resource in dealing with suppliers, service providers, and customers. However, if the employees are overly upset about the sale, making a clean, easy switch may not be easy.

Often, one of the best ways to encourage employees to support the new owners is to be open about the selling process and about what they can expect during and after the transition.

Some common questions an employee might have about the sale include:

- Will my job be safe?

- How involved will the previous owners remain, and for how long?

- Will my job responsibilities change?

- Who will be my new boss?

- What will change about our operating procedures?

- Will the working environment change?

- Will my pay and benefits remain the same?

- Will my work schedule stay the same?

- When will the change take place?

- How long has this been planned?

- Will all my coworkers still be here?

- Where will the old owner be going?

- Why did the owner decide to sell?

It is usually best to answer employee questions as honestly and openly as possible. Keeping the staff in the dark about what will happen will only make them suspicious.

If there are plans to change employee wages or benefits, make sure any new terms are clearly explained in writing.

Business Associates

Let anyone who has an ongoing business relationship with the store know about the change in ownership. Consider drafting a formal letter introducing the new owner and detailing the previous owner's role in the business, if he is going to have one. Consider sending a copy to the following people:

- Accountant

- Advertising/marketing consultant

- Account managers

- Suppliers

- Landlord

- Neighbors

- Printer

Have an attorney review any contracts the new business holds with suppliers, service providers, or subcontractors. A new contract may need to be drafted and the best time to know this is before the business has a need for inventory or support services.

Customers

If the retail establishment relies on repeat business, let returning customers know about the sale. Letting them in on the transaction can help make customers feel valued.

There are many approaches that can be taken to spread the word about the sale:

- **Mass marketing announcement:** Sending a post card to everyone in the customer database might draw some curious patrons – especially if a coupon is attached.

- **Personalized letter to patrons:** If extensive changes will be made to the business, a letter to the customers can help them know what they can expect.

- **Exclusive event:** If there is a concern that customers may be disappointed about the ownership change, consider hosting an event designed to lure them through the doors. Discounted merchandise, a presentation or workshops by someone who would interest clientele, or a sneak peak at the next season's inventory may encourage customer loyalty.

General Public

Make a public announcement about the sale only after employees, suppliers, service providers, and customers have been notified. If a customer who has been shopping at the store for years finds out about the change through an ad in the paper, their business may be lost forever. If an employee finds out the same way and takes out their frustration through bad customer service or malicious gossiping, 20 customers may be lost.

Here are some ways to let the general public know that there is a new owner of an existing retail business:

- **Signs at the store:** Simply displaying a "new ownership" sign outside the store may encourage customers to stop in so they can investigate any changes. If this strategy is chosen, be aware that visitors may ask employees for their opinions.

- **Advertisement:** An ad in the local paper is often an effective way to get the word out, not just about the transition but about the business in general. If a coupon is offered to celebrate the change, some new customers may visit the store.

- **Press release:** Sending a press release to the business section of the local paper does not guarantee publication, but if the paper does print the story it is free publicity. Those unfamiliar with writing press releases should consider hiring a freelance writer or use the following example.

SAMPLE PRESS RELEASE

Contact: Richard Riley
Tel. 999-999-9999   E-mail: r.riley@yournewstore.com

FOR IMMEDIATE RELEASE
CHANGES UNDERWAY FOR LOWERY FIBER ARTS

New Owner Wants to Continue Customer Service Tradition, Offer New Products

Since its establishment in 1976, Lowery Fiber Arts has provided local weavers, knitters, and needlework artists with supplies, equipment, and instruction.

That will not change, promises new owner Richard Riley.

"We will still be at the center of the traditional craft scene here in Lowery," says Riley. "We plan to offer the same top-of-the-line products and services LFA is known for, as well as an exclusive new line of luxury yarns.

Former owner Nancie Comfrey will continue teaching intermediate and advanced 4-harness weaving at Lowery Fiber Arts.

"I am only retiring from the business, not from the arts," says Comfrey. "I hope to see my old friends in the knitting room at LFA. I am looking forward to spending time there."

Lowery Fiber Arts will be hosting a workshop by award-winning quilter Barbara Sells on March 3. The public is invited to experience the new alpaca and cashmere blend yarns, Luxurique, at the open house after the workshop.

###

For more information or to schedule an interview, please contact Richard Riley at 999-999-9999 or e-mail r.riley@yournewstore.com.

Any business change, especially one as big as a new owner, is likely to cause some stress for the people involved. The following checklist can help make the transition smoother.

NEW OWNER CHECKLIST	
Transitioning Employees	
Inform about the sale prior to complete switchover.	
Inform about ongoing involvement of seller (if applicable).	
Discuss employee concerns.	
Distribute, in writing, any changes in employment terms.	
Distribute, in writing, any changes in store policies and procedures.	
Transitioning Business Associates	
Make a list of suppliers, service providers, and subcontractors	
With an attorney, review any contracts.	
Draft and send a letter regarding the change.	
Personally call associates as needed.	
Draft new contracts as needed.	
Transitioning Customers	
Decide on a strategy for publicizing change to customers.	
Implement strategy.	
Transitioning General Public	
Send a press release to business editor of local newspaper.	
Purchase an ad in local paper. Include a coupon if possible.	
Place a "new ownership" sign outside of store.	

8

BUYING A RETAIL FRANCHISE

If owning a retail business is appealing but the thought of coming up with a merchandise line, a logo, and a marketing plan is not, purchasing a franchise may be a good option.

WHAT IT MEANS TO OWN A FRANCHISE

When a franchise is purchased, an initial fee is paid, as well as royalties in return for the right to use the franchisor's trademark, products, and business system. Most franchises provide ongoing training and support for their franchisees.

Franchise or Business Opportunity?

In recent years, some multilevel marketing companies have labeled their business opportunities "private franchises." Unlike franchises, business opportunities usually allow sellers to operate under their own names rather than under the franchise name. Business opportunities have less expensive startup costs and do not place geographic market restrictions on sellers.

Advantages of Franchising

There are many benefits available to a franchisee that are not available to independent retail establishments. Some of the advantages of purchasing a franchise include:

- **Proven methods:** When a franchise is bought, a business game plan will be followed that has already succeeded in previous markets. Sales techniques, accounting software, purchasing procedures, and store policies will already be in place.

- **Better chance at success:** Franchisors want businesses carrying their names to succeed. Most will conduct extensive market, geographic, and competition analyses before selling franchises to potential franchisees. They may investigate if a potential franchisee has the necessary education, experience, resources, and personality to make the venture work. Be careful if a franchisor does not seem particular about where or to whom he places a franchise.

- **Defined image:** Franchises already have reputations. A customer who had a good experience at one location will transfer their loyalty to other businesses within the same franchise. Most customers will not even recognize the businesses as being separate.

Disadvantages of Franchising

Buying a franchise is not an easy or surefire way to retail success. There are many downsides to be a franchisee:

- **High initial costs:** Unlike starting a traditional business, when a franchise is purchased a franchise fee must be paid. This fee can be a few thousand dollars or up to several hundred thousand dollars, and it often does not include inventory and equipment.

- **Ongoing costs:** When a traditional business is started, suppliers, the mortgage, equipment rental fees, and service costs have to be paid. These expenses, on top of monthly royalty payments, are owed to the franchise company. With some franchises, the franchisee may also have to contribute to an advertising fund.

- **Limited future business opportunities:** Most franchise agreements include a non-compete clause, which would prohibit a franchisee from running a similar business. For example, if an arts and crafts franchise is purchased, the franchisee would not be able to run an independent yarn or art supply store in the future.

- **Not very independent:** Franchisees will be free to control many of the day-to-day operations of the business. They will get to schedule employees, decide on promotions, and determine how much to donate to local charities. Many of the big decisions, however, will be made by the franchisor. In order to promote conformity, most franchise companies decide on pricing, décor, design, and marketing strategies. The franchisor may even regulate where supplies come from and it may not be the vendor with the best prices.

- **The franchisor is in control:** If any of the terms of the franchise agreement are broken, the franchisor may terminate the contract. This means that if supplies are bought from a non-approved vendor, a royalty payment is missed, or an altered company logo is displayed, the entire investment may be lost.

TYPES OF RETAIL STORES AVAILABLE

There are franchises that sell nearly every type of retail good imaginable, including clothing, furniture, chocolate, craft supplies, toys, discount goods, fruit, and cosmetics.

Most retail franchise business models are brick-and-mortar stores, but some can be based out of the home. Many provide services such as delivery, consultations, and design, as well as retail sales.

HOW MUCH WILL IT COST?

The price to become a franchisee varies depending on the business chosen. Retail franchise startup costs can range from about $5,000 to over $500,000. Often, potential franchisees only have to have 10-50 percent of the startup costs in liquid capital. The franchisor or a third party can often provide financing.

FINDING THE RIGHT OPPORTUNITY

The first step to finding the right franchise investment is to consider personal interests. If the business relates to a personal interest, your business will be more enjoyable and have a better chance of success. The more experienced and knowledgeable the franchisee is in the industry, the more likely the franchisor is to approve the application.

Although the franchise company will provide training, certain skills cannot be taught. If a franchisee already has a passion for the merchandise, he or she will be a better business owner.

After interests are narrowed down, visit a franchise trade show. Often held in major cities, these shows give franchise companies a chance to show off their wares and talk to potential franchisees.

While at a franchise trade show, keep in mind the following goals:

- **Gather a list of possible franchise opportunities:** Try to find several franchises that would be fun to own. Determine if the time, resources, and skills necessary to be successful are reasonable.

- **Make a good impression:** It is never too early to start looking good as a franchisee applicant. Wear professional clothes, bring resumes and business cards, and show serious interest to the company representatives.

- **Make contacts:** Get to know the people working the booth. They are good people to get in touch with first if any questions arise about the company or the process.

- **Gather information:** Franchise sales representatives are required to present their Uniform Franchise Circular Offering (UFOC), which explains the franchise program and contains copies of the franchise agreement and the franchisor's audited financial statement. A sample pro forma operating statement should also be received.

After creating an initial list of possible franchise opportunities, research the options thoroughly. Read through the paperwork that was collected at the trade show. Ask an attorney to explain anything that is not understood.

Through the Internet, search for news articles about the companies. Research should be targeted toward answering the following questions:

- Is the franchisor profitable? What about current franchisees?

- How unique is the business model?

- Is the franchise credible?

- What is the success rate for franchisees?

- What kind of image does the franchise have nationally?

Research may turn up some red flags about the companies being investigated. The following warning signs do not necessarily mean that a franchise is fraudulent or a bad investment, but they may indicate a problem:

- **The company refuses to give you a UFOC:** Franchisors must provide a copy of the UFOC before a contract is signed or any money is paid. If a company says they are exempt from this requirement, odds are that they are a "business opportunity," not a franchise.

- **The company has been sued by numerous franchisees in the past:** Item three of the UFOC summarizes the franchisor's legal history for the previous ten years.

- **The franchisor or its officers have a history of financial problems:** Item 4 of the UFOC will list any bankruptcies.

- **The majority of the franchisor's revenue comes from selling supplies to the franchisees:** This information can be found in Item 8 of the UFOC. If the percentage is high, it may indicate that the supplies the franchisee is required to buy are overpriced.

- **The trademark is not federally registered:** Check Item 13 of the UFOC to see if the trademark registration is complete or pending. Pending registration may cause future problems.

- **Training is not provided:** Item 11 will detail the initial training requirements.

- **Any term listed in the UFOC does not make sense or does not seem fair:** It is a good idea to have an attorney who specializes in business law look over the UFOC.

The next step is to interview current and past franchisees for the companies of interest. The franchisor will make this easy, as Item 20 of the UFOC will contain the names and contact information of all franchisees that have joined and left in the past year.

Some of the questions to ask them are:

- Did the franchisor hold to the terms of the contract?

- Were the equipment, supplies, and inventory that the franchisee was required to buy from the franchisor of good quality and fairly priced? Were they delivered on time? Is the ordering process effective?

- Were the earning claims made on the sample operating statement indicative of the franchisee's earnings and performance?

- Has the franchisee had any disputes with the franchisor? How were they handled? What were the outcomes?

- Were there any undisclosed costs associated with starting or running the franchise?

- Was the training adequate? Did the franchisee feel confident getting started?

- What is the franchisee's overall impression of the company? Are they straightforward and responsible?

- Is the franchisee happy with his or her decision to purchase the franchise?

After finding a franchise that is interesting, seems to have a fair franchise agreement, and uses a viable business plan, it is time to review the actual franchise agreement and procure financing.

FINANCING A FRANCHISE

Most franchisors offer financing packages directly to franchisees. The packages available may include financing for the franchise fee, equipment, and operational costs. The franchisor may also help create a business plan and look for financial aid through banks and other outside lending institutions.

A franchise purchase may be eligible for an SBA guaranteed loan of up to $2 million. Getting an SBA guaranteed loan will not reduce the amount that needs to be repaid, but it may make a bank more likely to provide a loan if the franchisee's credit is not stellar. If a franchisee defaults on an SBA guaranteed loan, the government will pay back part of the debt. For more information at SBA loans, visit **www.sba.gov**.

A military veteran interested in buying a franchise may be able to take advantage of the International Franchise Association's Veterans Transition Franchise Initiative (VetFran) program. Franchisors that participate in VetFran offer veterans discounted initial fees.

9

STARTING FROM SCRATCH

For those who have an idea for a retail business that will be unique to the area and are the independent type who would rather build a company from the ground up, starting from scratch may be a good choice.

WHAT TO EXPECT

Unlike purchasing an existing store or franchise, starting a new retail business allows a person to make all the decisions from the very start. This can be exciting and overwhelming.

Advantages

One of the benefits to starting a new retail business is the opportunity to begin as small as desired. For example, a person who wants to sell handcrafted jewelry can run an online business from home after work. A franchise might have set hours that the store is required to be open, and an existing business might be too busy to run part-time, starting small provides an opportunity to learn the ropes, make mistakes, and determine if a business owner is the right choice without investing too much time or money.

Another advantage to opening a new, independent retail business is the chance to purchase inventory, supplies, and equipment from anywhere. If an existing business is purchased, the new owner will be stuck with the previous owner's choices until it is time for replacements. Franchisees have to buy at least some products from the franchisor. The ability to shop around may save significant money.

Starting a new business allows a person to choose the logo and name. The owner will be in charge of marketing strategies, branding, quality control, and customer satisfaction. He or she will get to set store policies and decorations. A franchising fee or royalties do not have to be paid and the owner gets to determine how much to put toward advertising.

Disadvantages

Of course, there is a downside to taking the independent route.

For starters, it is impossible to be an expert at all things. Large franchise companies can hire marketing professionals, graphic artists, and advertising gurus that an independent business might not be able to afford.

In addition, the owner of an independent business may end up spending time and energy developing procedures that franchise buyers are taught during their training. It may take a while to learn the most efficient processes. In the meantime, money, sales, and customers may be lost. The mistakes that a business owner makes can be very costly.

Franchisors will often help franchisees write business plans, create budgets, and approach lenders. Unless a business consultant is hired, the owner will have to do these tasks.

WHAT WILL I SELL?

No matter how clear the kind of inventory an independent retail store will carry may seem, it is likely that there is room to narrow the focus of the store. Having a good idea about what is to be sold will help the owner understand the market and recognized competitors — important steps toward finding a good location.

Whatever products are being considered, consider the following questions:

Are you interested in the merchandise?

It is hard to feign excitement over a product. If the owner is blasé about what is sold, how can customers be expected to be fascinated enough to spend their money?

Do you have experience with the merchandise?

It is impossible to tell the quality of the products unless something about them is known. The owner of a guitar store, for example, will need to be able to demonstrate models and attest to tone and craftsmanship.

Would you buy the product yourself?

If the owner thinks the inventory is ugly, low quality, or overpriced, odds are other people will too.

Is the merchandise available?

Unless the owner plans on making the inventory, reliable suppliers must be found.

Is the merchandise already everywhere?

On the other hand, if the merchandise is too easy to obtain, there may be stiff competition.

HOW MUCH WILL IT COST?

The cost of starting an independent retail business will vary according to the type of merchandise being offered and how the store is organized.

For example, an online store which sells print-on-demand reproductions of historical documents would have a much lower startup fee than a high end clothing store.

One of the advantages of starting a retail business "from scratch" is that the initial business concept can be tailored to fit within a budget. There is not a franchisor telling the owner what needs to be done or a seller setting a purchase price. The owner can start the business small, reinvest the profits, and grow.

CHOOSING A LOCATION

If a franchise is purchased, the franchisor will help the franchisee find a suitable site for the business. If an existing store is bought, odds are the business will not move right away.

By starting an independent retail store, the owner gets to decide on one of the most important factors that will contribute to the business's success — the location.

Why is the location so important? Because where the merchandise is sold will affect nearly every other aspect of the business, including:

- ✓ **Staffing:** Where the shop is located will influence what type of employees the store is able to attract and retain. If the owner wants suburban soccer moms to sell educational children's toys, it may take pretty high wages to lure them out of the suburbs. If the owner wants hip college kids to sell CDs, they may not have the transportation to venture very far from campus.

- ✓ **Image:** Customers will judge a book by its cover or a store by its location. If a high-end evening gown shop is in a rural strip mall between the farmer supply store and the surplus feed depot, it may be impossible to know how many women looking for elegant party dresses drove past the store, certain that nothing suitable could ever be found that far off the beaten path. Although it is possible to build a desirable image despite a less-than-desirable location, it usually depends on being lucky enough to attract a few good customers who will provide the store with free word-of-mouth advertising to the target market. Depending on luck is usually not the best strategy for a successful business.

✓ **Advertising:** If people do not routinely pass the store, more money will have to be devoted to tell them where it is. Instead of just convincing people to stop in, persuade them to take time out of their busy day to make a special trip to find the store.

✓ **Budget:** It may be tempting to go with the cheapest rent available, thinking that any image problems can be made up by having stellar merchandise. Be prepared to lose any savings to increased marketing and insurance costs. Going with the cheapest location usually does not pay off.

Understanding Your Target Market

In order to find a good location, it is important to have some idea about who the target market is. Although we will talk about marketing, image, and branding later in the book, be sure to think about the profile or the potential customer before deciding on a location.

Consider who would be most interested in the merchandise. Picture potential customers and think about the following questions:

– Will they likely be men or women?

– How old will they be?

– How much money do they make?

– Are they married?

– Do they have children?

– Will they be buying for themselves or for others?

– What other products or activities are they likely interested in?

– What kind of store would they like to buy from (upscale, discount, department)?

Finding Possible Locations

The first step in finding potential locations is to decide on a city. Most fledgling retail business owners assume they will open their store in the same town where they live, but that is not necessarily the best choice. When deciding on a town, keep in mind the following questions:

✓ **Is it close enough that the commute will not be dreaded?** A lot of time will be spent at the store. Try to find a place that is a comfortable drive.

✓ **Is the local population increasing?** A stagnant or declining population might not be able to support a business in the future.

✓ **Are there many people the same age and younger than the target market?** Start the business where there are plenty of people to sell to — now and in the future.

✓ **Are there many people in the same income bracket as the target market?** Be near people who can afford the merchandise.

✓ **Are there any stores in the area offering the same merchandise?** If there is too much competition for customers, look in another area.

✓ **Are services such as accounting, shipping, and printing available?** You will not want to interrupt a busy day at the store to make a long drive for routine services.

Finding the Information

Because so much of a retail business's success hinges on finding a suitable location, it is important to find out everything possible about an area before starting a store there. Two good sources of information about population demographics are the United States Census Bureau and independent research firms.

U.S. Census Bureau

Through the Census Bureau Web site, **www.census.gov**, information can be found about the household incomes, ages, and family sizes for communities across the country. One limit of the census data is that it is collected every ten years, so the information may be out of date.

Research Firms

Demographic research firms sell the same type of information that the Census Bureau provides, but they will often give more detailed data for a specific neighborhood. Their data may be more up-to-date than the information from the Census Bureau.

Choices, Choices

After deciding on a broad area in which to start a business, a commercial realtor can help find actual storefronts to start inspecting. Some of the following choices may be available:

- **Malls**

- **Strip malls**

- **Downtown**

- **Retail districts**

Review the potential sites for a new business using the following checklist.

POTENTIAL LOCATION CHECKLIST	
The site...	
is the right size for the business.	
is passed by an adequate amount of traffic.	
fits the image wanted for the store.	
would attract the target market.	
is near other businesses that are successful	
is near other businesses that cater to the target market.	

POTENTIAL LOCATION CHECKLIST		
has adequate parking.		
is visible from the road.		
is handicap accessible.		

Signing the Lease

A location that looks wonderful, would attract the target market, is convenient and well sized for the inventory may sound perfect. Unfortunately, an unfavorable rental agreement or a landlord who shirks his responsibilities can make a dream location turn into a nightmare.

Before signing a lease for a commercial property, ask the landlord these questions:

✓ How much is the security deposit? When can that be reimbursed? What are the reimbursement terms?

✓ Can the landlord offer a discount for the first six to twelve months, until the business is better established?

✓ How long is the lease for?

✓ When will the property be available? What condition will it be in? What if the property is not ready by that date?

✓ What rights will the landlord have to examine the property after the new owner takes possession?

✓ How will repairs be made? What recourse will the tenant have if repairs are not completed promptly?

✓ Does the landlord have any restrictions on signs?

✓ What changes is the landlord willing to make to the property?

✓ What changes will the tenant be able to make to the property?

✓ Will the tenant need to carry any insurance on the property?

✓ Will the landlord provide the new owner with the name and contact information of current tenants?

✓ What insurance does the landlord carry on the property?

✓ Who is responsible for maintaining the exterior of the property?

✓ Who, besides the tenant, will have access to the property?

✓ Are there any uses of the property that are prohibited?

✓ Can the rental agreement be transferred?

✓ What utilities are included in the rental agreement?

✓ What are the renewal terms for the lease?

✓ Who will pay the property taxes?

✓ If the property becomes damaged beyond use, will the tenant still be responsible for paying rent?

Make sure the answers to these questions are included in the lease agreement, as in the example.

COMMERCIAL LEASE AGREEMENT

This commercial lease agreement is entered into on February 17, 2005 between Johanna Smith ("landlord") and Sarah Hobbes ("tenant").

The landlord is the owner of the land and improvements at 7171 Cole Street, Reynoldsburg, Georgia and makes available for lease Suite C of the building, called the "Leased Premises" in this agreement.

TERM

The term of the lease shall begin on March 18, 2005 and end on March 17, 2010. The leased premises will be empty by the beginning of the lease. If the landlord cannot provide the leased premises by the agreed on date, the rent shall be abated for the length of the delay.

COMMERCIAL LEASE AGREEMENT

RENT

During the term of the lease, the tenant shall pay to the landlord rent of $22,800, payable in monthly installments of $1900. Each installment payment shall be due on the last day of each calendar month during the lease term. Installment payments shall be paid to the landlord at the following address:

717 Cole Street
Suite A
Reynoldsburg, GA

SECURITY DEPOSIT

The tenant shall pay to the landlord a security deposit in the amount of $1900 by March 17, 2005.

At the termination of the lease, if the tenant is not in default of the lease agreement and if the leased premises are in the same condition as they were at the beginning of the lease, the amount of the security deposit will be refunded to the tenant by a check delivered within two months of the termination of the agreement.

If any repairs to the leased premises are required, the cost of the repairs may be deducted by the landlord from the security deposit refund. In this case, an accounting of the use of the security deposit funds will be given to the tenant upon request.

UTILITIES

The landlord will pay all electricity, gas, water, and sewer charges on the leased premises. Arrangement for and payment of any other services are the responsibility of the tenant.

INSURANCE

The landlord shall maintain fire, flooding, and extended coverage on the property and leased premises. The tenant shall maintain comprehensive general liability insurance of not less than $1,000,000 per incident on the leased premises, a copy of which must be given to the landlord by March 17, 2005.

SIGNS

Any sign displayed at the leased premises and sized over 1 square foot must be approved by the landlord.

ENTRY

The landlord shall have the right to enter and inspect the leased premises, providing

COMMERCIAL LEASE AGREEMENT

such entry does not interfere unreasonably with the tenant's use of the leased premises.

TAXES

The landlord shall be responsible for property taxes associated with the property, excluding personal property taxes on the tenant's personal property at the leased premises, which shall be the tenant's responsibility.

REPAIRS, DAMAGE, and DESTRUCTION

Should the leased premises become damaged, though no negligence of the tenant or any agent, employee, or invitee of the tenant, and the leased property cannot be used for the tenant's purpose, then the tenant shall have 90 days from the date of the damage to elect and notify in writing to the landlord the termination of the lease.

In the event of minor damage to the leased premises through no negligence of the tenant or any agent, employee, or invitee of the tenant, the landlord shall promptly repair the damage. The cost of the repair shall be the responsibility of the landlord. The tenant shall be relieved of paying rent while the leased premises are damaged only for the length of time that business cannot be conducted in the leased premises.

DEFAULT

In the event the tenant defaults in the payment of rent to the landlord, the tenant shall have 30 days after receipt of written notice to cure the default. Should the tenant fail to cure the default within the time allowed, the landlord may declare the term of the lease ended by giving the tenant written notification of the termination.

CASE STUDY: TARA HANDKNITS AND HOT KNOTS

Sisters Gayle and Andrea Shackleton were not really looking to expand the retail side of their business. For 20 years they had been designing and making hand-knit clothing and wholesaling their products, as well as imports from a women's cooperative in Nepal.

"We had a studio sale once a year," says Gayle. "Besides that we only wholesaled."

Their plans changed when a historic building in Arcata, California became available.

"It was a great old building, with a façade and a lot of original features," says Gayle.

The sisters originally used the space as a studio outlet store. Eventually, to meet the demands of their market in the small, coastal town, they began offering other lines of clothes and dolls in addition to their original knits.

CASE STUDY: TARA HANDKNITS AND HOT KNOTS

"We were not really looking for a retail space," says Gayle. "But it seemed like the right thing to do."

Tara HandKnits and Hot Knots can be visited at 820 North Street in Arcata, California or on the Web at **www.hotknotsandtara.com**.

CHOOSING A NAME

After deciding on the type of retail goods to sell, learning a bit about the target market, and deciding on a location, it is time to choose a name for the business.

When crafting a name, there are several strategies that can be taken:

✓ **Be eponymous:** Show pride in the business – name it after its owner. By greeting customers with, "Welcome to *Joe's Gift Shop*, I'm Joe!" they will know they are in a one-of-a-kind place. Many people would rather shop in a store where the actual owner is behind the counter than at a large discount department store.

✓ **Use a pun:** Opening a craft store? How about *Knittin' Pretty*? A culinary supply shop? *Kneadful Things*. Even if a "punny" store name makes people groan, odds are that they will remember it.

✓ **Use the location:** Naming the store after the street it is on or a nearby landmark may make it easier for customers to find it and remember the location.

✓ **Be descriptive:** Not only does *The Little French Bakery* sound like a quaint and relaxing place, but no one will mistakenly go in there looking for auto parts.

✓ **Use alliteration or rhyme:** Repeated sounds often make a name memorable. For example, *Strings & Things* for a music shop, or *Planter's Paradise* for a garden supply company.

✓ **Appeal to the senses:** Some names just make people want to stop in, especially those that capture an inviting fragrance, texture, or sound.

Make a list of four or five names that are appealing. Practice saying them a few times with the following questions in mind:

✓ **Will this name be relevant later?** Hopefully the business will be around for a long time. A name based on current slang or trends might make the business appear outdated a few years down the road.

✓ **Will the target market feel comfortable saying the name?** To attract soccer moms, naming the business *Super Anarchy Punk House* might not be the best choice.

✓ **Is the name memorable?** Customers should be able to identify where they got such great merchandise and service. The owner does not want them to just call the store "some nice little shop downtown."

✓ **Is the name unique?** Do not get confused with the other "Corner Store" on another block.

✓ **Does it fit the image of the store?** The name is often the very first thing that starts building the tone of the business in customers' minds. Make sure it evokes the feelings desired. Being too cute, sophisticated, immature, or trendy might turn off some customers.

Many locations require special forms to be completed in order to operate a business under a fictitious name (also called a "Doing Business As" or *DBA*).

10

FINANCING YOUR BUSINESS

The next step in opening a business is to decide how much money is needed — and how it will be acquired.

Many business-owners shy away from financial planning. They think, or hope, that the money will take care of itself. While it is true that successful businesses have been founded on shoestring budgets, owners will not be doing themselves or their store any favors by skipping this section.

Creating a realistic budget will help calculate a reasonable startup cost. Knowing where the money is going can also lead to ideas for trimming expenses. If the estimated costs are too large or the budget cannot be followed, additional financing must be sought or the business structure must be changed before the problem becomes too large.

HOW MUCH MONEY WILL YOU NEED?

One of the most important things that can be done for a business is to have adequate funds from the start.

Initial business costs include more than just inventory and rent. Use the following worksheets to help establish how much working capital will be needed to get started. Not all businesses will require every listed expense.

At the very minimum, access to enough money to keep the business afloat for a month will be needed. This is very optimistic and assumes that the business will bring in the revenue to cover its operating expenses almost right away.

The total calculated is the minimum that should be secured before starting the business. If the store is like most, a large profit will not be seen at first. Until the pricing, marketing, and inventory details are worked out, the business may be operating at a loss.

The following worksheet will help calculate a startup number that will give the business more wiggle room for incidental and unexpected expenses — which may mean less stress if things do not go exactly as planned.

MINIMUM STARTUP COSTS	
Description	**Estimated Cost**
Property Expenses	
Deposit	
First month's rent	
Merchandise Expenses	
Initial inventory	
Business Insurance (one quarter)	
Legal Expenses	
Franchising fee	
Trademark licensing	
Business license	
Fictitious name ("DBA") paperwork	
Corporation/Partnership agreement	
Communication Expenses	
Telephone installation	
Web site address registration	
Web site hosting, monthly	
Internet access, monthly	
Equipment and Supplies	
Vacuum cleaner	
Cleaning supplies	
Office supplies	
Delivery vehicle	

MINIMUM STARTUP COSTS	
Shelving and displays	
Computer and software	
Cash register	
Point-of-sale system	
POS subscription, monthly	
Personal Expenses	
Lost wages (if leaving a job) for three months	
Health insurance, quarterly	
Personnel Expenses for one month	
Wages	
Advertisements for employees	
Training	
Taxes	
Health Insurance	
Marketing Expenses	
Outdoor signs	
Advertisements	
Interior Design Expenses	
Carpeting	
Interior signs	
Paint	
Furniture	
Decorations	
Other Expenses	
TOTAL	$

TYPES OF FINANCING

Determining a realistic estimate for the startup costs associated with opening a retail business can be daunting. It may seem impossible to save that much money.

A **personal contribution** to the business includes any money that comes from personal paychecks, savings accounts, or investments. This also includes computer equipment, vehicles, and merchandise that are currently owned but that will be used to support the business venture. Franchises and loan officers often require a substantial personal contribution, as having the money on hand demonstrates that a person is financially able to invest in his or her own business.

Credit cards offer one of the easiest and quickest ways of obtaining startup funds. Many credit card companies now offer "small business" cards that provide discounts at office stores. They usually have few requirements and a simple application process — which makes them attractive to the new business owner who seems to be wading through a sea of paperwork. Most suppliers accept credit cards, making them a convenient way of paying for inventory.

Be careful using credit cards or lines of credit for startup funds. It is an easy way to "nickel and dime" a large balance. For those planning to start a sole proprietorship or partnership be especially weary, because the owner will likely be responsible for any charges accumulated, even if the business is closed.

Grants are gifts from a funding source that do not have to be paid back. Companies, state and local governments, and nonprofit organizations can be sources of grants for startup companies. To be eligible for some grants, certain income or personal criteria must be met.

Most grant providers want to be assured that their money is going to the right business. They want to be connected with a successful endeavor, so be prepared to make the case that the money will be used wisely and responsibly. The application process may be complex and demanding — it will help to have the business plan mapped out before starting.

Some grants may require frequent audits or progress reports. The grants may be revocable if the money is not being used as reported or if the funding organization dissolves. In addition, some grant agencies may offer, or require, workshops on business practices, marketing strategies, and accounting. Some may require community service from business owners that are given grants.

Many retail businesses are partially funded through **loans**. Loaned money must be repaid. Opportunities for business loans may be available from local governments, banks, individuals, and nonprofit agencies. The Small Business Administration (SBA) offers programs to help fledgling businesses secure loans.

Because lenders want to be paid back, the application process for a business loan can be extensive. Lenders will want to check on the owner's private credit rating, savings, and income, to assure that the money will be paid regardless of how the business does.

INTERNAL FUNDS

Before deciding where to go for money, it is essential that a business has a clear picture of how much money will be needed from external sources.

The first step is calculating how much the owner himself will have to invest in the business. Many lenders prefer to deal with businesses that are primarily owner-funded. Not only does it show that the owner has the ability to save enough money to start a business, but it suggests that the owner believes strongly in the viability of the business. Lenders may think that if there is a substantial personal contribution, the owner will be more likely to persevere and work hard to make the store profitable.

Personal savings is the first place to look for personal contribution funds. A financial advisor can help determine the long-term and short-term consequences of pulling money out of different types of accounts. A monthly budget can help the owner see how much money can be put into the business on an ongoing basis.

The following worksheets will help determine the owner's personal financial contribution to the business.

PERSONAL FINANCIAL CONTRIBUTION	
Description	**Amount**
Initial Investment	
From savings	a.
From other investments	b.
Ongoing Contributions	
Monthly investment times 12	c.
Total Personal Contribution (add a, b, and c)	

Now use the total from the Estimated Startup Cost Worksheet to determine how much money is still needed.

ESTIMATED STARTUP COST SHORTFALL	
Description	**Amount**
Estimated Startup Costs	a.
Personal Financial Contribution	b.
Shortfall (subtract b from a)	

Seek external or additional internal funds to compensate for any estimated startup cost shortfall. Otherwise, review the Estimated Startup Cost Worksheet to see where the business may be able to scale back, at least temporarily. Can the business be run completely on the Internet for a while, saving on property expenses? Can the store be run while keeping a job to reduce lost wages and health insurance costs? Even a part-time job can help defray the expense of starting a retail business.

FINDING FUNDS

The time to start researching where the money for the business will come from is before the first employee is hired, before a lease is signed, and even before a business plan is written.

The amount of money that can reasonably be expected at startup is one of the most important factors in determining location, marketing strategy, and inventory. It is never too soon to start looking at the funding sources available.

Finding More Internal Funds

The personal contribution may already be calculated, but more money may be needed to reach the estimated startup costs. It might help to look at raising more money. Is there anything that can be sold or any service that can be provided to help bring in more funds? Can a part-time job be taken for a few months, applying the earnings to the startup costs?

Finding External Funds

Local business schools and chambers of commerce are good places to start looking for business grants. Associations and advocacy groups tied to ethnic background, gender, profession, or interests may also offer, or have information about, grants and loans.

For those who think they will need a business loan to startup or at some point during the early operations consider scheduling an initial interview at a local bank. A consultant at the lending department may be able to give advice about how to improve the chances of securing a loan.

Visit **www.sba.gov** for information about SBA-guaranteed loans. The local SBA office may have information about special purpose grants and lenders who are friendly to startup companies. The SBA may also be able to connect the owner with a mentor to help with the financing process.

Although it is never too early to start researching funding sources, most lending and grant programs will require a more in-depth financial analysis of the business when an application is filled out. We will cover the break-even analysis, income projection, and budget analysis when preparing the business plan.

11

WRITING A BUSINESS PLAN

A business plan is the blueprint for a company's future. This document will help define goals and tactics for marketing, finances, and organization. With one, it is possible to tell if the business is on track or where changes need to be made. Without one, time may be wasted with ineffective marketing strategies and opportunities may be missed to save money on inventory, rent, services, or supplies.

Most lenders will want to see a business plan before they approve a business loan. Not only does the financial section help them determine if the business is a good credit risk, but the fact that this crucial document has been prepared will show professionalism. The time and effort put toward creating a business plan reflects how serious the business venture is being taken.

WHEN SHOULD YOU BEGIN?

A formal business plan may not be composed until many of the details of the company are ironed out. A location and a name must be decided and the business structure must be finalized.

However, it is never too early to start constructing an informal business plan. Keep this plan in a three-ring binder with each section clearly labeled and stocked with notepaper and a pocket. Jot down any notes and ideas in the appropriate section. File copies of any business documents collected, such as the lease agreement and business license.

Crafting a business plan often shows holes in the preparation. This is usually a good thing— when problems are known, they can be corrected.

When it is time to write a formal plan, preferably before the first sale, it will be much easier if notes and documents are organized.

WHAT WILL YOU NEED TO BEGIN?

The type of retail business being opened and whether or not an existing store is being purchased will determine what paperwork is needed before beginning. Before writing a business plan, try to gather as many of the following documents as possible.

Owners' Resumes: Unless the business is incorporating or will have partners, the owner will just need to have his or her own resume updated. Include educational background, work experience, professional affiliations, and special skills. Any retail, management, or marketing experience should be added to the resume.

Owners' Financial Statements: This is the personal assets, liabilities, income, and expenditure. Most lenders will want this information from a new business owner. Determining one's personal financial position will also help decide how much can be invested in the new business.

Credit Reports: Thanks to the Fair and Accurate Credit Transactions Act (FACT Act), one free personal credit report can be received from each of the three largest credit reporting agencies — Experian, Equifax, and TransUnion — every 12 months. More information about free credit reports can be found at **www.AnnualCreditReport.com**. If a business is already owned, check with Dun & Bradstreet (**www.dnb.com**) about obtaining a business credit rating.

Location Report: Potential financiers will want to know that a viable home has been picked for the business. The details of the business location may be useful for crafting the business plan.

Franchise Agreement: If a franchise is being opened, be sure to be able to refer to the rules about how the business can and cannot be marketed.

Copies of the Lease/Mortgage: These will be needed for the budget.

Licensing Agreements: If a product, logo, or service is being licensed, the licensing agreement will likely have rules about marketing, use, and distribution.

List of Existing Inventory and Assets: Whether an existing business has been bought or inventory has been produced or purchased, know what the business already owns. Vehicle titles and large equipment registration papers should also be included.

Market, Population, and Demographics Research Reports: One of the first steps of creating a marketing plan is defining the target market. These documents will help determine who will most likely buy the product.

Competition Report: In writing the marketing portion of the business plan, develop tactics to differentiate the business from the competition. The more information gathered about them, the easier that task will be!

Preliminary Balance Sheet: This document shows what the business owns and how much operating money it has. The more the business already has through personal contribution, the more seriously lenders tend to take the application.

References: Some financiers will require letters of reference. Now is the time to ask at least two business associates, suppliers, or customers to write a letter attesting to the owner's reputation and reliability.

Current Loan Papers: Gather the latest statements from any business or personal lines of credit or loans.

Articles of Incorporation/Partnership Agreements: Unless the owner is a sole proprietor, an agreement specifying the role of each owner is needed. Keeping this agreement in mind while writing the business plan can save grief and misunderstanding later.

Business Licenses: Creditors will want to know that the owner is registered with the appropriate government agencies.

"Doing Business As" Paperwork: In most areas a "Doing Business As" or DBA, form will be needed. Filing a DBA allows credit to be established and bank accounts to be started under a fictitious name, most likely the store's. This does not mean the owner is not financially responsible for accounts under the DBA, but it does help brand the store.

Insurance Policies: Financiers will want to know that their investment will not be lost to a fire, flood, accident, or lawsuit. Budget for the premiums.

Not only will having these documents on hand for reference help craft a business plan, but lending institutions may want to see them if outside funding is sought.

GENERAL WRITING GUIDELINES

When writing a business plan, try to remember the "three C's": complete, clear, concise.

Complete: Add as much detail as possible to the plan. Avoid vague statements like, "We will market effectively." What strategies will be employed? Who will be marketed to? Why was that tactic chosen? Details are critical. Not only do they show financiers that thought was put into the plan, but details are what will make the business plan a useful tool for developing the company.

Clear: Do not use flowery phrases or technical jargon hoping to impress potential investors. This is a common tactic and other business people are likely to see right through it. If asking for a loan or credit, it is the owner's responsibility to convince the lender that the business is a good risk and that the lenders are likely to get their money back. This will not be accomplished by hiding behind three and four syllable words. Funds will not be granted until the people in charge of reviewing the business plan completely understand how the business will be run. The best bet is to make their job as easy for them as possible.

Concise: This is a business document. Banks do not care if Great-Uncle Horace always wanted to sell motorcycle accessories. Most likely, it is not important that your 15-year-old daughter thinks the store sounds great and wants to work there on weekends. Unless personal background, anecdotes, hobbies, or opinions have a direct correlation with the target market, leave it out of the business plan.

PARTS OF A BUSINESS PLAN

Following the accepted format for a business plan will help lenders find the information they need quickly. The time to be creative is when developing and marketing the business, not in organizing the written business plan.

The business plan should include a cover sheet, table of contents, executive summary, organizational plan, marketing plan, financial documents, and supporting documents.

Cover Sheet

The cover sheet will introduce the business to prospective lenders. It should include the name, address, and logo of the company, as well as the contact information for the owners or corporate officers. The bottom of the cover sheet should include who wrote the business plan and when it was prepared.

Table of Contents

The table of contents is a navigation tool for the reader. Try to make it as clear as possible. Do not overuse watermarks, fancy fonts, or graphics. Most word processing programs include tools to help create a table of contents after the document has been written.

Executive Summary

The executive summary boils the business plan down to the most essential elements. At a minimum, someone should be able to read the executive summary and find out:

- ✓ The name, location, and owners/officers of the company.

- ✓ The legal structure of the company.

- ✓ The products the company sells.

- ✓ How long the company has been in business.

- ✓ Who manages the business.

If the business plan is being used for a loan application, include:

- ✓ How much money is needed and what it will be used for.

- ✓ What collateral is offered.

- ✓ When repayment can begin.

It is usually easier to write the executive summary after the rest of the business plan has been completed.

Organizational Plan

The organizational plan will go into detail about the following aspects of the business:

- ✓ **Legal Structure:** Is the business a sole proprietorship, partnership, or corporation? Why was this structure chosen as the best for the business? Who are the owners or officers of the business and what are their qualifications?

- ✓ **Personnel:** How many employees will there be and what will they be paid? Who will manage different business operations, and why are they qualified? Include an organizational chart.

- ✓ **Products:** What will be sold? Who will be the suppliers? How will the products be sold? Through a store? Catalog? Web site? How much inventory will be carried?

✓   **Insurance:** Who will provide insurance for the business? What is covered and for how much? What security measures are being taken to protect the assets?

✓   **Accounting:** Describe the accounting system. Will independent audits be conducted? If so, describe the schedule.

Marketing Plan

As the owner of a retail business, become familiar with the concepts and tools related to marketing. The details of the marketing plan may need to be updated often in response to changing market trends, customer demands, and growing experience.

Using marketing to increase sales is addressed in the *Marketing and Advertising* chapter. To get started crafting a basic initial marketing section for the business plan, think about the retail business goals, analyze the market, and develop some broad strategies for meeting the goals.

Goals

The first section of the marketing plan should list the goals for the company. All the marketing efforts should focus on meeting one or more of these goals.

It is important to define what the business wants to accomplish through its marketing strategy; otherwise, it cannot be determined if the money, time, and energy are paying off.

Some examples of marketing goals are:

✓   **To increase sales to return customers.** It usually costs more to bring a new customer to the door or Web site than to have a customer come back. By increasing sales to return buyers, the profit margin may increase.

✓ **To increase Web site hits.** In order to buy online, potential customers have to first visit the Web site.

✓ **Increase brand recognition.** If the business is offering something new or improved, the target market should become more aware of the existence and benefits of the products.

A business's goals may differ from the examples. When writing marketing goals, try to avoid the obvious "sell more merchandise." Think about what would have to happen to move more inventory. Will more customers have to come through the door? Sell more products to each customer? Increase catalog distribution? Bring more people to trunk sales?

Market Analysis

The market analysis section lists details about the target market, market trends, and competition.

The first step is to define the demographics of the target market. Think about the potential customers and the following characteristics:

✓ age	✓ family size
✓ gender	✓ marital status
✓ income	✓ home ownership status

Next, think about what motivates the customer. What are they looking for in their purchases? Some examples include:

✓ status	✓ quality time with family
✓ safety	✓ child development
✓ prestige	✓ professional development
✓ self-improvement	✓ niche merchandise
✓ health	✓ niche hobby accessories

How can this information be found? The United States Census Bureau (**www.census.gov**) and independent marketing research firms can help. Interviews, questionnaires, surveys, and focus groups can also help to better understand the target market.

Include an analysis of the competition in this section. Competitors may include:

✓   Businesses selling the exact same products.

✓   Businesses selling similar products.

✓   Businesses selling to the target market.

In the analysis, discuss what separates the business from its competitors. Why would customers buy the products over the competition's? Why would the target market spend their money at the shop instead of at a competitor's?

Strategies – How will you meet your goals?

Forming marketing strategies can be one of the most creative parts of owning a retail business. There is no limit to what can be done to meet marketing goals. Here are some examples using the model goals above:

✓   **To increase sales to return customers.**

    ✓   With each sale, give the customer a coupon for ten percent off the next purchase.

    ✓   Offer a customer loyalty program. Customers who spend $100 get a $20 gift certificate.

    ✓   Increase customer service. Call each regular customer by name. Offer all visitors a cup of coffee while they browse.

✓   **To increase Web site hits.**

    ✓   Request links on Web sites related to the merchandise.

✓ Provide free online articles, tools, forums, and other resources.

✓ Write articles for consumer magazines related to the products. Include the Web site address in the biographical information.

✓ **Increase brand recognition.** If the business is offering something new or improved, make the target market more aware of the existence and benefits of the products.

   ✓ Give talks to groups of interest to the target market. Make sure to mention the product and what makes it unique.

   ✓ Buy advertisements in consumer magazines and Web sites to spread the work about the product.

   ✓ Support a local charity or neighborhood event related to the target market.

Financial Documents

There are many financial documents that might be included in this section of the business plan.

   ✓ If an existing business has been bought, include the *balance sheet* and *profit and loss statement.*

   ✓ If a franchise is being purchased, add the pro forma income documents provided by the franchisor, as well as any budget projections specific to the business.

   ✓ If a new independent business is being started, a projected *balance sheet, profit and loss statement,* and *break-even analysis* will be needed.

   ✓ If the business plan is being created as part of a loan application package, include a summary of financial needs and a breakdown of how the loan money would be used.

Supporting Documents

Any documents used to define the organizational plan, develop the marketing plan, or calculate any financial documents can go in this section. These may include:

- ✓ insurance policies
- ✓ contractor estimates
- ✓ contracts
- ✓ credit reports
- ✓ leases
- ✓ letters of reference

- ✓ product descriptions from suppliers
- ✓ product rate sheets from suppliers
- ✓ resumes of owners or officers
- ✓ questionnaires or surveys
- ✓ demographic reports

Do not include original documents in the business plan; always use copies.

FORMATTING AND PACKAGING THE PLAN

When packaging the business plan, remember the three C's. Keep it *complete*, *clear*, and *concise*.

- ✓ **Complete**

  - ✓ All sections are written.

  - ✓ Important information is included.

  - ✓ Margins, fonts, and styles are consistent throughout.

- ✓ **Clear**

  - ✓ The business name and logo is printed neatly at the top of each page.

✓ The pages are numbered.

✓ The table of contents includes page numbers to make information easy to find.

✓ The print is dark and readable.

✓ **Concise**

✓ The finished business plan should be about 30-40 pages long.

✓ Major points should be listed in the executive summary.

Here are some other points to keep in mind when packaging the business plan:

✓ Keep the working copy of the business plan in a three-ring binder, but have copies included in loan applications professionally bound.

✓ Using excessive colors, graphics, and fonts may make the plan look unprofessional.

✓ Using glossy paper or an expensive cover may seem wasteful.

✓ Have someone else read through the business plan to look for typos and other errors. The business plan should put forth the image of quality and professionalism.

UPDATING YOUR BUSINESS PLAN

As the business continues to develop and grow, it is likely that the business plan will need to be changed. Do not think of this document as merely a way to obtain funding. If updated regularly, it can be an important resource if the owner decides to expand the business, change the inventory, or create a new marketing plan.

SAMPLE BUSINESS PLAN

BUTTERNUT GARDENING SUPPLIES, A HOME-BASED BUSINESS SEEKING A BUSINESS LOAN

Executive Summary

Butternut Gardening Supplies is a sole proprietorship established in 2003 in Philadelphia, Pennsylvania. The mail-order and online retail sales company is seeking working capital in the amount of $18,000 to set up a seasonal retail location at the Triadelphia Shopping Plaza from April through August.

The $18,000 loan will enable *Butternut Gardening Supplies* to purchase additional inventory and display fixtures.

Repayment of the loan can begin within one month of receipt of the funds.

Butternut Gardening Supplies is owned and operated by Sarah Devlin. Devlin holds graduate degrees in business and horticulture from Carnegie Mellon University.

Organizational Plan

Description of Business

Butternut Gardening Supplies has offered unique gardening tools, supplies, clothing, and accessories through its catalog and the Internet since 2003. Based in Philadelphia, Pennsylvania, the company targets affluent hobby gardeners looking for items that are prettier and more durable than what they can find at their local home improvement stores.

The company has sold to customers around the world. Over 50 percent of our customers order again within the year.

The *Butternut Gardening Supplies* Web site averages over 400 hits per day. Approximately two percent of these translate into sales. On average, buyers spend $138 per transaction.

Legal Structure

Butternut Gardening Supplies is a sole proprietorship owned and operated by Sarah Devlin, MS, MBA. We are currently restructuring as a Limited Liability Corporation. The restructuring should be completed by February of this year.

Personnel

In addition to the owner, *Butternut Gardening Supplies* currently employs three employees:

SAMPLE BUSINESS PLAN

BUTTERNUT GARDENING SUPPLIES, A HOME-BASED BUSINESS SEEKING A BUSINESS LOAN

Customer Service Representative: part-time at $9 per hour.

Duties:

- Answer telephone calls and e-mails for company.
- Process online and catalog orders.
- Gain familiarity with product line.
- Understand company policy about customer service.
- Provide customer service as dictated by company policy.

Technical Manager: part-time at $11 per hour.

Duties:

- Maintain and update the company Web site.
- Maintain and update company computer equipment.
- Train affiliated artists to use our order fulfillment software.
- Answer any technical questions from affiliated artists.

Artist Liaison: part-time at $15 per hour.

Duties:

- Find new artists of interest to *Butternut Gardening Supplies*.
- Contact affiliated artists about special requests or customer service issues.
- Maintain good relationships with affiliated artists.

All employees report to the owner.

In addition, the following employees will be hired to work at the Triadelphia Shopping Plaza retail site:

Site Manager: part-time at $13 per hour.

Duties:

- Open store.
- Verify sales figures and reconcile discrepancies.
- Handle any customer service issues at the Triadelphia Shopping Plaza site.
- Write work schedule.
- Be knowledgeable about product line.

SAMPLE BUSINESS PLAN

BUTTERNUT GARDENING SUPPLIES, A HOME-BASED BUSINESS SEEKING A BUSINESS LOAN

Sales Consultant: part-time at $9 per hour.

Duties:

- Handle sales transactions at Triadelphia Shopping Plaza site.
- Gain familiarity with product line.
- Understand company policy about customer service.
- Provide customer service as dictated by company policy.

Management

I, Sarah Devlin, am the manager and sole proprietor of *Butternut Gardening Supplies*. As you can see from my resume, I earned graduate degrees in business and horticulture from Carnegie Mellon University. In addition, I have worked at independent and chain garden supply stores and greenhouses throughout high school and college.

I started *Butternut Gardening Supplies* to meet an unmet need I saw in the gardening community. Gardeners wanted tools and accessories that other gardeners would envy.

Since starting *Butternut Gardening Supplies,* I have continued my education by taking classes in accounting and retail management through the Small Business Association (SBA).

I am currently in contact with three advisors with backgrounds in marketing, accounting, and business law. My marketing advisor is Cynthia Marlowe, a consultant with UBG Marketing in Philadelphia. *Butternut Gardening Supplies'* accountant is Julio Sanchez of Sanchez Accounting in Philadelphia. For legal counsel, we retain Henrietta Long of Long, Cottle, and Mormar in Pittsburgh.

Products

The product line of *Butternut Gardening Supplies* consists of hand-painted, limited edition gardening tools, supplies, clothing, and accessories.

The company currently carries only a very small inventory for immediate shipping. Most of the orders are fulfilled on-demand by specialty artists and craftspeople. Orders are usually fulfilled and shipped to the customer within three weeks of purchase.

Butternut Gardening Supplies currently works with over 50 artists and craftspeople, mostly in the Appalachian region. They are chosen for the quality and uniqueness of their work.

SAMPLE BUSINESS PLAN

BUTTERNUT GARDENING SUPPLIES, A HOME-BASED BUSINESS SEEKING A BUSINESS LOAN

Insurance

Carrier: Brook Street Insurance

567 Brook Street

Philadelphia, PA

(555) 678-9101

Agent: John Loren

Type of Insurance:

Business/Personal: $300,000

Deductible: $ 5,000

Liability: $500,000

Premium:

Annual Premium: $6000

Monthly Premium: $ 500

Security

- *Butternut Gardening Supplies* equipment is kept locked inside the office. Only the owner has a key to the company office.

- The few pieces of inventory held by the company at any time are stored in a locked cabinet inside the office. Only the owner has a key to the cabinet.

- Triadelphia Shopping Plaza will provide a locked storefront for the retail site. The Plaza will also provide around the clock security. Only the owner and site manager will have copies of the key for the retail site.

- In order to prevent shoplifting and walk-in theft at the retail site, three closed-circuit monitoring cameras will be installed.

Accounting

All bookkeeping is done by Sarah Devlin using *QuickBooks*™. Julio Sanchez, CPA, of Sanchez Accounting in Philadelphia handles tax accounting and financial reporting.

SAMPLE BUSINESS PLAN

BUTTERNUT GARDENING SUPPLIES, A HOME-BASED BUSINESS SEEKING A BUSINESS LOAN

Marketing Plan

Goals

Butternut Gardening Supplies goals for this fiscal year are:

1. To welcome at least 200 visitors per day to our seasonal retail site at the Triadelphia Shopping Plaza.

2. To average at least 50 transactions per day at the Triadelphia Shopping Plaza site.

3. To have an average transaction price of at least $75 at the Triadelphia Shopping Plaza site.

4. To increase the number of daily hits to the company Web site by 15 percent.

5. To increase the average size of transactions through the Web site by 15 percent.

Our long-term goals are:

6. To increase traffic, transaction number, and average size of transactions at the Triadelphia Shopping Plaza site by 10 percent each year.

7. To increase traffic, transaction number, and average size of transactions through the company Web site by 10 percent each year.

8. To increase the percentage of customers in the 18-24 age bracket to 10 percent (up from 4 percent) and in the 25-44 age bracket to 25 percent (up from 11 percent) within five years.

Market Analysis

1. Target Market

   1.1. Profile

      - **Demographics:** *Butternut Gardening Supplies* customers are mostly female, aged 45-65, with an average household income of over $100,000.

      - **Work:** Most of our customers are retired or part-time professionals or business owners.

SAMPLE BUSINESS PLAN

BUTTERNUT GARDENING SUPPLIES, A HOME-BASED BUSINESS SEEKING A BUSINESS LOAN

- **Habits:** Our customers are avid gardeners or buy gifts for gardeners. Many are competitive horticulturalists. They tend to shop at high-end retail stores.

- **Location:** Through its catalog and Web site, *Butternut Gardening Supplies* has sold to customers across the world. However, a majority of our customers are located in the New England states.

1.2. Retail Location

The Triadelphia Shopping Plaza is home to several high-end retail stores. A recent survey performed by the Plaza's marketing team found that the average shopper there is 52, female, with an average household income of $120,000. Furthermore, 39 percent of their shoppers indicated "gardening" as a hobby.

1.3. Market size

Butternut Gardening Supplies sends catalogs to over 25,000 customers each year. In addition, our "opt-in" e-mail database consists of nearly 116,000 addresses.

The Triadelphia Shopping Plaza welcomes about 5,000 customers everyday.

1.4. Other factors

Butternut Gardening Supplies has exclusive contracts with many of their artists, assuring that most of the inventory cannot be bought anywhere else.

2. Competition

2.1. Competition for mail order/online sales

There are no other online or mail order stores offering the same selection of decorated tools and accessories as *Butternut Gardening Supplies*. A few of the artists do sell their work through other venues, such as their own Web sites, other retailers, or craft shows.

2.2. Competition at Triadelphia Shopping Plaza site

The Triadelphia Shopping Plaza site is approximately two miles from a large home improvement store. However, *Butternut Gardening Supplies* does not expect much overlap in clientele. Instead, the main competition is expected to come from the other specialty stores at the Plaza:

SAMPLE BUSINESS PLAN

BUTTERNUT GARDENING SUPPLIES, A HOME-BASED BUSINESS SEEKING A BUSINESS LOAN

- **Just in Thyme** – botanical-based toiletries and decorations

- **Well Chosen** – antique home and personal accessories

- **Final Touches** – fine and costume jewelry

- **Patty's** – imported gifts

3. Market Trends

    "Outdoor Living Takes a New Twist in 2007"
    From: *The Garden Media Group*
    Date: August 25, 2006
    Summary: More homeowners are investing money in creating elegant gardens with dominant accessories.

    "2006 Summer Gardening Trends Research Paper"
    From: *The Nursery and Landscape Association*
    Date: June, 2006
    Summary: Homeowners are spending more time in their gardens. Over half of Americans want to use their gardens for relaxation.

    "Is Your Advertising Targeting Your Best Potential Customer?"
    From: *The Nursery and Landscape Association*
    Date: Spring, 2003
    Summary: Customers in the 18-25 age bracket are most likely to plan to spend more on gardening. Container gardening is becoming increasingly popular, especially in higher income homes.

Strategies

Butternut Gardening Supplies will be implementing the following strategies to reach its marketing goals:

1. To welcome at least 200 visitors per day to our seasonal retail site at the Triadelphia Shopping Plaza.

    - Send direct mailings publicizing the site to customers in the database who are local to the area.

    - Display outdoor signs at the Plaza and a billboard on the main road.

SAMPLE BUSINESS PLAN

BUTTERNUT GARDENING SUPPLIES, A HOME-BASED BUSINESS SEEKING A BUSINESS LOAN

- Distribute flyers at local greenhouses.

2. To average at least 50 transactions per day at the Triadelphia Shopping Plaza site.

- Train sales staff in suggestive selling techniques.

3. To have an average transaction price of at least $75 at the Triadelphia Shopping Plaza site.

- Train sales staff in up-selling techniques.

- Offer "buy one get one half off" sales on selected merchandise.

4. To increase the number of daily hits to the company Web site by 15 percent.

- Distribute online sales literature and coupons at the Triadelphia Shopping Plaza site.

- Increase *Google™ AdWords* budget by 15 percent.

5. To increase the average size of transactions through the Web site by 15 percent.

- Offer more bundled merchandise choices.

- Start a "Buyer's Rewards" program, where customers can earn $1 in credit for every $15 spent.

- Increase selection of higher priced merchandise.

6. To increase traffic, transaction number, and average size of transactions at the Triadelphia Shopping Plaza site by 10 percent each year.

- Build local customer information database by 20 percent each year.

- Send out direct mailings reminding local customers of our yearly re-openings.

- Move from a seasonal location to a permanent retail site within four years.

- Offer free horticulture classes and workshops at retail location.

7. To increase traffic, transaction number, and average size of transactions through the company Web site by 10 percent each year.

SAMPLE BUSINESS PLAN

BUTTERNUT GARDENING SUPPLIES, A HOME-BASED BUSINESS SEEKING A BUSINESS LOAN

- Increase *Google™ AdWords* budget by 10 percent yearly.

- Add value-added service options to the Web site, included expedited handling, signed pieces, customization, and gift wrapping.

8. To increase the percentage of customers in the 18-24 age bracket to 10 percent (up from 4 percent) and in the 25-44 age bracket to 25 percent (up from 11 percent) within five years.

- Add two artists with a more modern, industrial aesthetic to the company.

- Consult a graphic artist about updating the print material and Web site to appeal to a younger age group.

- Add a blog and discussion board to the Web site.

Financial Documents

Use of Loan Funds

Butternut Gardening Supplies will use the $18,000 loan as follows:

DISPLAY FIXTURES (SEE ATTACHED PRICE LIST)	
2 large hanging racks @ $350	$700
2 8' shelving units @ $1,470	$2,940
3 10' shelving units @ $1,500	$4,500
Paint and decorations	$830
POS system (seasonal rental)	$1,580
Retail space security deposit	$1,500
Inventory	$5,950

In addition to the loan, owner Sarah Devlin will be investing $45,000 of her personal funds toward the purchase of additional inventory and startup costs. This will give the retail site a starting inventory worth $45,590 wholesale. The approximate retail value of this inventory is $76,425 (see attached price list). We suggest this inventory as collateral for the loan.

Quarterly Budget

SAMPLE BUSINESS PLAN

BUTTERNUT GARDENING SUPPLIES, A HOME-BASED
BUSINESS SEEKING A BUSINESS LOAN

Budget Item	1/05-3/06	4/06-6/06	7/06-9/06	10/06-12/06
Sales/Revenue				
From Catalog	1,204	1,745	1,908	3,200
From Web site	97,152	98,256	100,464	104,880
Less Costs of Goods				
Purchases	49,177	52,000	52,186	64,848
Gross Profits	49,178	48,001	50,186	43,232
Variable Expenses				
Advertising/Marketing	2,067	2,345	4,567	6,201
Catalog Printing		526		528
Gross Wages	10,440	10,216	10,987	13,861
Shipping	8,352	9,651	7,435	1,213
Miscellaneous	431	357	668	974
Depreciation	31	31	46	46
Fixed Expenses				
Accounting	320	320	320	320
Legal	170	145	145	145
Insurance	1,500	1,500	1,500	1,500
Worker's Comp	209	204	220	277
Supplies	148	189	190	176
Telephone	75	75	76	79
Internet	16	16	16	16
Misc.	82	93	118	94
Total Expenses	23,841	25,668	26,288	25,430
Net Income from Operations	25,337	22,333	23,898	17,802
Other Income				
Other Expenses (Interest)	1,756	1,975	1,156	1,458
Net Profit (Loss) Before Taxes	23,581	20,358	22,742	16,344

SAMPLE BUSINESS PLAN

BUTTERNUT GARDENING SUPPLIES, A HOME-BASED BUSINESS SEEKING A BUSINESS LOAN

Profit and Loss Statement

PROFIT AND LOSS STATEMENT

Starting Date: 1/1/2006		Ending Date: 12/31/2006
INCOME		
Income From Sales		408,808
b. beginning inventory		
c. purchases	218,211	
d. C.O.G. available sale (b+c)	218,211	
e. ending inventory (on ending date)		
Cost of Goods Sold (d-e)		218,211
Gross Profit on Sales (IFS-COGS)		190,597
EXPENSES		
f. advertising/marketing	16,234	
g. freight	23,650	
h. order fulfillment	3,001	
i. packaging	2,430	
j. wages	45,504	
k. travel		
l. depreciation (product assets)		
m. other variable (not fixed) expenses		
Total Variable Expenses (add f through m)		90,819
n. insurance and worker's comp	6,910	
o. salaries		
p. licenses	387	
q. rent		
r. utilities	369	
s. administrative costs	1,885	
t. depreciation (equipment)	154	
u. other fixed expenses	703	
Total Fixed Expenses (add n through u)		10,408

SAMPLE BUSINESS PLAN

BUTTERNUT GARDENING SUPPLIES, A HOME-BASED BUSINESS SEEKING A BUSINESS LOAN

PROFIT AND LOSS STATEMENT

Starting Date: 1/1/2006		Ending Date: 12/31/2006
Total Operating Expenses (TVE + TFE)	154	
Net Operational Income (GPS - TOE)		88,370
aa. interest income		
bb. interest expense	6,345	
Net Profit Before Tax (NOI + aa - bb)		83,025
cc. federal taxes	29,059	
dd. state taxes	16,605	
ee. local taxes	4,151	
Total Taxes (cc + dd + ee)		49,815
NET PROFIT/LOSS AFTER TAXES (NPBT-TT)		33,210

BALANCE SHEET
AS OF: 12/31/2006

ASSETS		LIABILITIES	
Current Assets		**Current Liabilities**	
Cash and Equivalents	12,056	Accounts Payable	698
Petty Cash	512	Accrued Liabilities	
Receivables		Accrued Income Taxes	
Inventory	113	Long-Term Debt, due within one year	3,670
Prepaid Expenses		Capital Lease Obligations, due within one year	
Other Assets			
TOTAL CURRENT ASSETS	12,681	TOTAL CURRENT LIABILITIES	4,368
Property and Equipment			
Buildings, Improvements		Long-Term Debt	2,366
Fixtures, Equipment	4,065	Long Term Capital Lease Obligations	
Transportation Equipment		Deferred Income Tax	

SAMPLE BUSINESS PLAN

BUTTERNUT GARDENING SUPPLIES, A HOME-BASED BUSINESS SEEKING A BUSINESS LOAN

BALANCE SHEET
AS OF: 12/31/2006

ASSETS		LIABILITIES	
Total Property and Equipment, at cost	4,065	Other	
Less Depreciation	1,684		
Net Property and Equipment	2,381		
Property under Capital Lease			
Less Amortization			
Net Property Under Capital Lease		OWNER'S EQUITY	8,328
Goodwill			
Other Assets			
TOTAL ASSETS	15,062	TOTAL LIABILITIES	15,062

PRO FORMA CASH FLOW STATEMENT FOR TRIDELPHIA SITE, YEAR ONE

	Start Up	April	May	June	July	August
Beginning Cash Balance	45,000	3,070	1,231	566	582	1,009
Sales Revenue		18,236	20,060	22,066	24,272	26,699
Cost of Goods Sold	45,590	13,677	15,045	16,549	18,204	20,024
VARIABLE EXPENSES						
Marketing/Advertising	200	2000	200	200	200	200
Gross Wages	1,015	2,012	2,012	2,012	2,012	2,012
Shipping						
Misc.	12,050					
TOTAL VARIABLE	13,265	2,212	2,212	2,212	2,212	2,212
FIXED EXPENSES						
Insurance & Worker's Comp	175	210	210	210	210	210

SAMPLE BUSINESS PLAN

BUTTERNUT GARDENING SUPPLIES, A HOME-BASED BUSINESS SEEKING A BUSINESS LOAN

PRO FORMA CASH FLOW STATEMENT FOR TRIDELPHIA SITE, YEAR ONE

	Start Up	April	May	June	July	August
Rent	650	650	650	650	650	650
Supplies	250	100	100	100	100	100
Utilities						
Loan Repayment		750	750	750	750	750
TOTAL FIXED	1,075	1,710	1,710	1,710	1,710	1,710
Interest Expense						
Federal Taxes		921	369	169	174	302
State Taxes		460	185	90	88	151
Local Taxes		1,094	1,204	1,324	1,456	1,602
TOTAL CASH OUT	59,930	20,074	20,724	22,050	23,844	26,002
Cash Balance	-14,930	1,231	567	582	1,010	1,706
Loans to be Received	18,000					
ENDING CASH BALANCE	3,070	1,231	567	582	1,010	1,706

PRO FORMA CASH FLOW STATEMENT FOR TRIDELPHIA SITE, YEAR TWO

	April	May	June	July	August
Beginning Cash Balance	1,706	1,017	2,775	4,356	5,901
Sales Revenue	29,369	32,306	35,537	39,090	43,000
Cost of Goods Sold	22,027	24,230	26,653	29,318	32,250
VARIABLE EXPENSES					
Marketing/Advertising	200	200	200	200	200
Gross Wages	2,012	2,012	2,012	2,012	2,012
Shipping					
Misc.	1,580				
TOTAL VARIABLE	3,792	2,212	2,212	2,212	2,212

SAMPLE BUSINESS PLAN

BUTTERNUT GARDENING SUPPLIES, A HOME-BASED BUSINESS SEEKING A BUSINESS LOAN

PRO FORMA CASH FLOW STATEMENT FOR TRIDELPHIA SITE, YEAR TWO

	April	May	June	July	August
FIXED EXPENSES					
Insurance and Worker's Comp	210	210	210	210	210
Rent	650	650	650	650	650
Supplies	100	100	100	100	100
Utilities					
Loan Repayment	750	750	750	750	750
TOTAL FIXED	1,710	1,710	1,710	1,710	1,710
Interest Expense					
Federal Taxes	512	305	833	1307	1770
State Taxes	256	152	416	653	885
Local Taxes	1,762	1,938	2,132	2,345	2,579
TOTAL CASH OUT	30,059	30,547	33,956	37,546	41,407
Cash Balance	1,017	2,775	4,356	5,901	7,494
Loans to be Received					
ENDING CASH BALANCE	1,017	2,775	4,356	5,901	7,494

PRO FORMA CASH FLOW STATEMENT FOR TRIDELPHIA SITE, YEAR THREE

	April	May	June	July	August
Beginning Cash Balance	7,494	7,606	10,147	12,533	14,933
Sales Revenue	47,299	52,029	57,232	62,956	69,251
Cost of Goods Sold	35,475	39,022	42,924	47,217	51,938
VARIABLE EXPENSES					
Marketing/Advertising	200	200	200	200	200
Gross Wages	2,012	2,012	2,012	2,012	2,012
Shipping					
Misc.	1,580				

SAMPLE BUSINESS PLAN

BUTTERNUT GARDENING SUPPLIES, A HOME-BASED BUSINESS SEEKING A BUSINESS LOAN

PRO FORMA CASH FLOW STATEMENT FOR TRIDELPHIA SITE, YEAR TWO

	April	May	June	July	August
TOTAL VARIABLE	3,792	2,212	2,212	2,212	2,212
FIXED EXPENSES					
Insurance and Worker's Comp	210	210	210	210	210
Rent	650	650	650	650	650
Supplies	100	100	100	100	100
Utilities					
Loan Repayment	750	750	750	750	750
TOTAL FIXED	1,710	1,710	1,710	1,710	1,710
Interest Expense					
Federal Taxes	2,248	2,281	3,044	3,760	4,480
State Taxes	1,124	1,141	1,522,	1,880	2,240
Local Taxes	2,838	3,122	3,434	3,777	4,155
TOTAL CASH OUT	47,187	49,489	54,846	60,556	66,735
Cash Balance	7,606	10,147	12,533	14,933	17,449
Loans to be Received					
ENDING CASH BALANCE	7,606	10,147	12,533	14,933	17,449

Supporting Documents

Competition Comparison

TRIADELPHIA SITE COMPETITION ANALYSIS

This data was obtained by observing stores' sales activity over the course of three weeks and analyzing their catalogs and Web sites.

	Just in Thyme	Well Chosen	Final Touches	Patty's	Butternut Gardening Supplies
Product Line	Botanical-based toiletries & decorations	Antique home and personal accessories	Fine and costume jewelry	Imported gifts: perfumes, accessories, and jewelry	Unique gardening tools, supplies, clothing,& accessories

SAMPLE BUSINESS PLAN

BUTTERNUT GARDENING SUPPLIES, A HOME-BASED BUSINESS SEEKING A BUSINESS LOAN

TRIADELPHIA SITE COMPETITION ANALYSIS

	Just in Thyme	Well Chosen	Final Touches	Patty's	Butternut Gardening Supplies
Average Customer Gender	Female	Female	Female	Female	Female
Approximate Average Customer Age	25,35	35-45	34-45	25-35	45-65
Approximate Average cost of merchandise	$15	$45	$150	$9	$70
Entrance	Inside plaza only	Inside plaza only	Inside plaza only	Inside plaza only	Inside and external plaza entrances
Online Presence	No	No	Yes, no sales	Yes, no sales	Yes, including sales
Image	Inexpensive, trendy gifts and impulse purchases	Casual chic	Business professional	Highly discounted bargains	Unique, high quality accessories for the serious garden hobbyists

After studying and comparing the competition at the Triadelphia Shopping Plaza site, the management of *Butternut Gardening Supplies* believes that the store can sufficiently differentiate itself due to the following:

- There is little overlap in the average customer age of the existing gift and specialty stores at the plaza and those of *Butternut Gardening Supplies*.

- *Butternut Gardening Supplies* sells merchandise at price points that are not serviced by the current Plaza stores.

- There is no overlap in the merchandise that will be carried by *Butternut Gardening Supplies* at the Triadelphia site and the inventory of the other stores there.

SAMPLE BUSINESS PLAN

BUTTERNUT GARDENING SUPPLIES, A HOME-BASED BUSINESS SEEKING A BUSINESS LOAN

Owner's Resume

Sarah Devlin
P.O. Box 867
Philadelphia, PA
555-123-4567
sdevlin@butternutgardening.com

Qualifications

Since I started *Butternut Gardening Supplies* in 2003, the business has grown to have over $400,000 in annual sales. I continue to learn about business, horticulture, and the hobbyist gardener through continuing education classes and through my involvement with the *American Horticulture Association.*

Education

M.B.A.
1996: Carnegie Mellon University
Completed courses in management, marketing, information systems, and business law. Graduated with a 4.0 GPA.

M.S. Horticulture
1992: Carnegie Mellon University
Completed an independent research project on selective breeding of rhododendrons. Presented papers at regional and national conferences. Taught undergraduate level biology and horticulture laboratory classes.

B.S. Horticulture
1990: University of Pittsburgh
Coursework included plant pathology, biogeography, botany, and greenhouse business. Graduated *summa cum laude.* President of botany, biology, and horticulture clubs. Invited to participate in undergraduate research in horticulture laboratory.

Relevant Experience

Retail Manager
1996-2003: *Poppalong Horticulture and Greenhouse*
Philadelphia, PA
Scheduled crew, resolved customer and employee concerns. Ran inventory. Helped select merchandise.

SAMPLE BUSINESS PLAN

BUTTERNUT GARDENING SUPPLIES, A HOME-BASED BUSINESS SEEKING A BUSINESS LOAN

Retail Sales Crew
1991-1996: *L and L Greenhouse*
Balmore, PA
Helped customers select plants, tools, and accessories. Learned about needs and wants of the avid hobbyist gardener.

Letter of Recommendation

Bette MacDougal
Owner, *Poppalong Horticulture and Greenhouse*
P.O. Box 976
Philadelphia, PA
(555) 765-4321

To Whom It May Concern:

I have known Sarah Devlin in a professional capacity for over ten years. I have never known anyone so organized, qualified, and determined to succeed in the horticulture industry.

For six years, Sarah managed my store, *Poppalong Horticulture and Greenhouse*. Under her direction, our annual sales grew by over 15 percent each year. She always treated the staff with respect and made sure everyone was fully trained and competent in their position.

After Sarah started *Butternut Gardening Supplies*, we were excited to partner with her new business for workshops, sales, and other promotions. Sarah always ran these events the same way she runs her business – with complete organization and an eye for the bottom line.

Sarah has always understood the serious horticulturist. She knows what makes them tick and the product line at *Butternut Gardening Supplies* shows that. Many of my customers come in bragging about their new "Butternut find," eager to show off their one-of-a-kind tool, shirt, or garden decoration.

It has been very exciting for me to watch Sarah's business grow over the years. I know she has big plans for the business and will continue with her success.

Sincerely,
Bette MacDougal
Owner, *Poppalong Horticulture and Greenhouse*

12

BEFORE YOU OPEN

By the time a business format has been decided on, a business plan has been written, and financing has been secured, the owner will already have gotten a taste of just how much work "being your own boss" actually is.

OPENING A BUSINESS BANK ACCOUNT

Retail business owners will be dealing with frequent monetary transactions. Even before the first sale, inventory may need to be bought, filing fees must be paid, and deposits on equipment must be put down.

It is a good idea to separate business funds from personal expenses from the very start. One way to do this is to open a business checking account.

Consider the following when choosing a bank for handling a business account:

- **Does the bank handle night deposits?** Those planning on closing their store after normal banking hours will not want to have the cash register sitting full until morning.

- **Does the bank handle the credit card services needed?**

- **Does the bank offer a change service?**

- **Is there a branch nearby?**

- **Are the bank employees helpful and courteous?**

- **Is the bank small and local?** It may be easier to secure a loan through a small bank that has been servicing a customer's needs for years, rather than a large bank where a person is just another account.

- **What are the fees for the services most likely to be used?**

After deciding on a bank and opening an account, be sure to order:

✓ Checks

✓ Deposit slips

✓ Coin wrappers for change

✓ Night deposit bags and keys

✓ Bank envelopes

SUPPLIERS

Unless all the goods being sold are made by the owner, odds are the business will have to work with one or more suppliers. Suppliers sell goods at bulk or wholesale rates. Finding suppliers is not hard, but finding good ones can be a challenge.

Often, suppliers will mail a business a catalog or call after a business license is applied for. Wholesalers can be found by researching on the Internet, attending a trade show, or asking other retailers in the same industry.

If a business knows the brand of merchandise it wants to sell, the manufacturer can either act as a supplier or put the business in contact with authorized distributors.

What to Look For

One of the most important things to do to keep from getting scammed by dishonest sellers is to be educated. Be able to recognize what determines quality in the goods being sold. Be able to recognize counterfeits and be familiar with brands and pricing.

Be sure to research any potential suppliers before placing an order. How long have they been in business? Do they seem to understand the products they are selling? Are the prices in line with the industry? Where are they located? Do not be afraid to ask for and check out references.

Maintaining a Good Relationship

When some honest and reliable suppliers have been found, be sure to keep them. Treat suppliers with respect — do not waste their time, handle any problems calmly, and pay bills on time. If a new supplier offers a better deal on merchandise, consider giving the current vendor the chance to match the price.

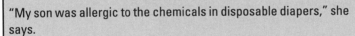

CASE STUDY: DRYBEES

Lisa Adkins started DryBees because of her own disappointing experiment with cloth diapers.

"My son was allergic to the chemicals in disposable diapers," she says.

"I purchased old-fashioned pre-fold diapers, but hated how bulky they were. I started to cut on them and make them look more like a disposable diaper. Through trial and error, I had diapers for my son that I really liked. I liked them so much that I started making and selling them online."

She started selling diapers sewn from about five yards of extra fabric. She now purchases over 8,000 yards of material every month.

"I used to choose my suppliers based on how nice they were on the phone and their prices. I have realized that not all good suppliers are nice on the phone. I have learned that when you get nasty suppliers on the phone you just have to be very aggressive. Perhaps this is their way of weeding out the weak?"

Lisa has found that her image is one of the best marketing tools.

"I have to be very careful that my image is clean in all aspects," she says. "It is a small world and when I am on the Internet I am always representing my business, even if I am discussing politics on a state forum."

For more information about DryBees, visit **www.drybees.com.**

DEVELOPING A PRODUCT LINE

Deciding what a store is going to carry can be one of the most fun aspects of owning a business, but it can also be one of the most frustrating. If too little merchandise is bought, the store will look bare. Too much and it will be crowded. Would customers rather have several different types of things to choose from, or many variations within the same category? Just how much should be charged for the goods?

When developing a product line, remember to go slow, keep good records, and do not be afraid to experiment. Do not be afraid to make mistakes; they are often the only way to really understand the market.

How Many Different Categories of Merchandise Should You Sell?

Say the owner is planning to open an independent bookstore. Maximizing profits is desirable, of course. That may mean selling to as many people as possible. With that assumption in mind, a business may be tempted to carry all sorts of books: best sellers, classics, fad diets, travel resources, computer manuals, home improvement guides, etc.

Unfortunately, for many small businesses that strategy can easily backfire. If only one or two books are in stock on parenting or foreign language, the inventory may seem puny. Customers might decide to go where they will have a bigger selection.

A general rule of thumb for developing a product line is, "If you cannot do it justice, do not do it." If handcrafted jewelry is being sold, do not display a single necklace. Wait until there are several for the customers to choose from. If pet supplies are being sold online, wait until there are at least three or four leashes, collars, or chew toys before creating a separate Web page for dog accessories.

How Many Varieties Should You Offer?

Most customers enjoy choices. They like buying products that reflect their personalities and preferences. Most of the time, stocking several varieties of the same merchandise is a good business move. When customers touch items to compare the quality and features, they are more likely to purchase one.

How Much Should You Charge?

Retail business owners are almost constantly looking for the perfect price for their merchandise – the highest number they can put on the price tags and not scare customers off.

There are many factors that need to be considered when pricing products:

- **Supplier costs** – Determine how much the merchandise costs the business, including shipping and insurance. Some retailers calculate a percentage of the wholesale price and add that markup to their costs in order to determine what they will charge.

- **Competitors' prices** – It is important to know what other retailers are charging for similar merchandise. Some retailers deliberately undercut other stores or offer to beat or match their prices, hoping to draw budget-conscious customers. Others price a little higher than their competitors, hoping that customers will be willing to pay extra because of the store's image.

- **Perceived value** – What customers think of a product, manufacturer, or store influences what they will be willing to pay. "Prestige makeup," available only at high-end department stores, is often ten or 20 times more expensive than the drugstore lines.

- **Added value** – People may be willing to pay more for the same merchandise if they feel they are getting something extra. Customers may prefer buying from a small local store where the owner stands behind the products, even if it is more expensive than at a large online retailer where returning a purchase might mean spending hours on the telephone. Staff expertise is another quality that patrons might pay more for, especially if salespeople take the time to help them pick out the most suitable model.

- **Overhead** – A retail business is opened in order to make money, so do not forget to allow for overhead expenses when setting prices. Overhead includes rent, utilities, loan payments, and employee wages.

- **Price points** – As more experience is gained selling to the target market, it may be found that certain price tags are more likely to move merchandise, almost regardless of what that merchandise is. Perhaps it is discovered that little ornaments near the cash register sell quickly when they are priced at $4.95, that gift items go well at $25.50, or that parents cannot resist wooden toys at $14. If prices work well, they are often effective starting points when pricing new merchandise.

Finding the prices that maximize profits will likely take some experimentation. Keeping good records and analyzing sales data often will help set prices that are fair to customers and help the bottom line.

DECORATING AND RENOVATING

Whether starting a retail business from scratch, buying an existing store, or becoming a franchisee, odds are the desired building, exactly as imagined, will not be waiting to be rented or bought. In order to get the look and functionality needed for the store, some redecorating or renovating may need to be done.

Renovations

Extensive renovations can be a tricky and expensive process. If there is a limited startup budget, consider only performing the remodeling necessary to make the retail space safe, accessible, and functional.

The owner may be tempted to save money by doing the renovations himself or herself. Those who are especially handy may feel comfortable tackling small jobs such as fitting laminate flooring, replacing doors, or installing shelves. Larger plumbing, construction, or remediation problems often require the expertise of a professional. Using a contractor from the beginning can save money and frustration. Contractors will often help navigate any regulations which may need to be followed for extensive renovations.

If the business space is being rented, be sure to get the landlord's approval before making any permanent changes.

Many areas have special rules in place to protect the integrity of historic buildings. Those planning to alter the outside appearance of the building should check the local ordinances to make sure any neighborhood covenants will not be broken.

Be familiar with applicable construction codes and handicap accessibility requirements. Following regulations and building "to code" from the beginning is usually cheaper than having to correct problems later.

Retail Layouts

One of the first decisions to make about the store is what floor plan to use. A good sales floor layout accomplishes several objectives, including:

✓ Making shoplifting more difficult.

✓ Helping the merchandise look its best.

✓ Encouraging shoppers to look at all the displays.

There are several simple floor plans to choose from and endless variations on these basic designs. The best one for a business will depend on the physical dimensions of the space and the type of inventory being sold.

Straight Layouts

Straight layouts feature shelves, racks, or other display elements positioned either perpendicular to or parallel with the store's walls.

Straight layouts can allow for more storage in a small area while still leaving ample aisle space.

One disadvantage of this type of floor plan is that the displays can provide nooks where customers cannot be seen from the counter. This may increase losses due to shoplifting. Because of this, straight layouts are most often seen in jewelry stores, where the inventory is secured within locked cases.

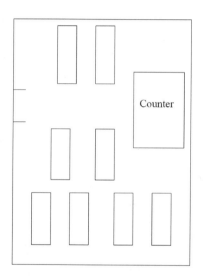 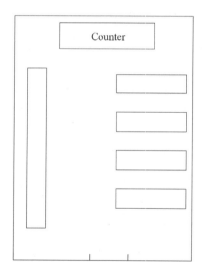

Diagonal Layouts

With diagonal layouts, shelves are positioned at an angle to the store walls. Like straight layouts, quite a bit of merchandise can fit in a small area.

The angles in a diagonal layout help open up the view of the store from the cash register, which may result in less loss. This layout is particularly well-suited to merchandise that is displayed in cases or shelves, but can be adapted to clothing hung from racks.

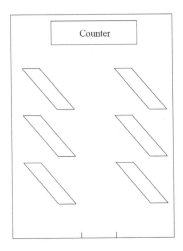

Staggered Layout

Another way to position the display elements is to stagger them throughout the sales floor. This helps encourage customers to meander throughout the store, looking at each display.

The staggered layout is not the most efficient use of space, but it is a good way to call attention to small collections of merchandise. It is most often used in upscale clothing or gift shops.

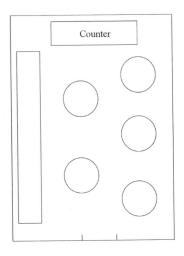

Geometric Design

A geometric design combines a straight layout with a staggered layout. The most common implementation of this technique is to put less expensive items on the straight displays and the higher end merchandise on the smaller, staggered displays. This lets a business to fit more budget or clearance items at one end of the store while reserving room to show off the more impressive collections.

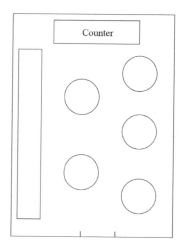

The "U" Layout

The "U" layout is a straight design where shelves line three walls of the store with the sales counter positioned in the middle. This gives the sales staff a full view of the store, allowing them to help customers promptly. It also provides wide aisles and encourages customers to look over the entire inventory.

This layout can often be seen in jewelry stores, where the staff needs to be available to unlock cases for potential customers.

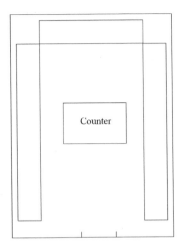

The Geometric "U" Layout

The "U" layout can also be employed by wrapping the sales counter with individual displays. This floor plan allows a business to fill up space with little inventory. It is often used in stores selling formal wear or handcrafted items.

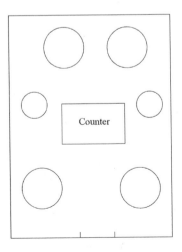

Decorating to Reflect Your Image

Before investing money in furnishings, accessories, and decorations, spend some time thinking about a color scheme for the retail space. Ask the following questions:

- **How should customers feel when they walk through the door?** Certain colors seem to help people recall specific moods, emotions, and memories. Green, for instance, suggests reliability, safety, and freshness. Blue gives a feeling of tranquility and calmness. Black seems sophisticated. Red is passionate.

- **Will the colors work with the logo?** Consider placing some signs around the store. They should not clash with the décor.

- **Are there suitable materials available in the colors?** Decorating elements that fit with the store's image will be needed. Make sure they are available before committing to a color scheme.

- **Are the colors likeable?** The owner will be spending quite a bit of time in the store and should make certain he or she will feel comfortable.

- **Will the colors work with features that cannot be changed?** If new flooring cannot be installed, make sure the color scheme coordinates with the carpet or tile.

- **Do the colors work with each other?** If the owner cannot decide between teal and orange, should both be used? Not necessarily. Adjacent colors influence each other and some perfectly beautiful hues may be overwhelming when placed together. There are many color theory resources available, but in the end what matters most is how well the color scheme works. Paint some large patches of wall or hang up a few yards of cloth. Live with the colors a few days and be sure they look good beside each other.

After a palette has been decided on, begin assembling decorating accessories. Depending on the store size, what will be sold, and personal preferences, consider some of the following:

✓ Posters	✓ Wallpaper
✓ Vases	✓ Stencils
✓ Flowerarrangements	✓ Statues
✓ Wall hangings	✓ Lamps
✓ Pillows	✓ Clocks
✓ Table runners	✓ Portable electric fireplace
✓ Paint	✓ Window treatments
✓ Area rugs	

There are many places to find accessories. Those on a limited budget should check out thrift stores, auctions, and closeout stores. There are also warehouses and suppliers who will sell commercial-quality decorations directly to businesses. Home improvement stores often have a wide selection of decorative items.

Before buying any decoration, check the quality and suitable of the item.

- **Is it safe?** Make sure that any lamps or other electrical devices are UL-listed. Items should not have chipped paint or small pieces that children can put in their mouths. Glass decorations are prone to shatter and should be placed carefully if used.

- **Is it durable?** Even if something is cheap, if it needs to be replaced often it might not be such a good buy.

- **Does it fit the color scheme?** Do not be afraid to have one or two contrasting pieces, but make sure they are different enough that they do not just look like mistakes.

- **Does it fit the store's image?** If the store is trying for a sophisticated look, a worn out sofa will be at odds with the desired image.

- **Will it coordinate with other decorations?** If the posters feature jungle scenes, chintz drapes may clash.

- **Does it detract from the merchandise?** The products should be the stars of the store. The décor should enhance the shopping experience, but not be the focus.

- **Is it a good value?** What if an antique quilt that blows the decorating budget but would look perfect in the retail space? Try to put a price value on how much the quilt would add to the store's appearance. Think about it in terms of other elements. Is it worth less lighting? Cheaper window treatments? Staying with the current wallpaper?

Decorating can be a large, time consuming, and expensive task. Luckily, most of the time the space will not have to be perfectly decorated before opening the store. Improvements, updates, and additions can continue as long as the store stays open.

A good way to keep from being overwhelmed by the task of decorating the store is to take an inventory of what tasks are most desirable, and then rank the tasks according to importance. What must be done before the store opens? What should be the very next priority? What would be nice as time and money allow?

Use the following worksheet as an example for organizing a decorating plan.

DECORATING NEEDS				
Area	Current Description	Desired Improvement	Estimated Cost	Priority N=Now S=Soon E=Eventually
Sales Floor				
Wall Treatment	Chipping, dingy, white paint	New, yellow paint with blue trim	$450	N
Floors	Carpet over hardwood	Pull up carpet and redo hardwood floors	$800	N
Window Treatments	No window treatment	New drapes, shades, and valances	$1,250	N

DECORATING NEEDS				
Wall Accessories	None	10 framed posters	$850	N
Shelf Accessories	None	Coordinating bookends and ornaments		S
Lighting	Overhead	Display lights for each shelf	$1,000	N
Other		Area rug for checkout desk	$750	E
Public Restroom				
Walls	Chipping, dingy, white paint	New blue paint	$200	N
Floors	Old vinyl tile	New vinyl tile	$700	E
Window treatments	None	New valences	$150	S
Fixtures	Adequate, plain	Update	$450	E
Accessories	None	Install toilet paper holder, soap dispenser, and hand dryer	$300	N
Other		New "restroom" sign	$45	S
Employee Room				
Walls	Chipping, dingy, white paint	New paint	$200	E
Floors	Adequate			
Window Treatments	None	New drapes	$300	E
Fixtures	None	Install lockers	$200	E
Accessories	None	Table and chairs	$400	N
Other		Small refrigerator and microwave	$400	S
Storage Area				
Walls	Chipping, dingy, white paint	New paint	$200	E
Floors	Adequate			

DECORATING NEEDS				
Window Treatments	Shades, adequate			
Accessories	Some bins, dirty	New bins, stackable with drawers	$750	E
Fixtures	Small overhead light	Install fluorescent lights	$350	E
Other				

If the thought of decorating the store is overwhelming, or if the owner cannot trust his or her creative eye to tell if the choices are working, consider hiring a professional interior decorator.

Many decorators have inside sources and may be able to get better deals on supplies and services. Even if the budget is small, a professional decorator may be able to demonstrate techniques and give suggestions that will help save money.

Equipment

If a brick-and-mortar retail store is being opened, some sort of equipment or fixtures will be needed. For example, the following might be needed:

- Shelves to store excess inventory
- Display fixtures
- Mannequins
- Desks

- File cabinets
- Counters
- Cash registers
- Vacuum cleaner

All equipment that is bought should meet the following criteria:

- **It should be safe.** This is a cardinal rule for anything that is brought into the business.

- **It should be sturdy.** Durable equipment is often less expensive in the long run.

- **It should fit the store.** Being able to move around is key, even in storage rooms.

- **It should be able to grow with the business.** Keep in mind that other units may be added as needed.

In addition, equipment that will be seen by customers should also:

- **Enhance the image of the business.** If country crafts are sold, milk crates and rough, hewn planks may be a good choice. If fine jewelry is being sold, however, they may look cheap.

- **Coordinate with the décor.** Do not just throw together a collection of furnishing because they happen to be available and fit into the budget. Even if up every piece does not match, try to make sure that they look good together. One way to do this is to create a unifying element between all the pieces. Can they all be painted the same color? Replace all the tops with the same surface? Use the same knobs and handles throughout the store?

- **Show the merchandise at its best.** The display fixtures can enhance the merchandise or take away from it. For most types of inventory, make sure the products are well-lit and on a contrasting background.

- **Be proportional to the sales area.** Any equipment in the showroom should fit with the physical characteristics of the store. Do not stuff huge furnishings in a tiny space. Customers should feel comfortable and have room to browse.

Equipping the retail space can be an expensive endeavor. Look for bargains in these places:

- **Other businesses:** Some businesses upgrade their equipment often. If another store is being remodeled or renovated, there may be good deals on their old equipment.

- **Auctions:** Private and business auctions can be a great place to find used equipment. The purchases will usually be "as is", but high quality pieces may be found for a fraction of their new cost.

- **Retail stores:** Retail furniture and equipment stores may be able to provide substantial price breaks on floor models or discontinued pieces.

- **Business supply stores:** Most business supply stores offer a huge selection of commercial-quality equipment. The sales representative may be able to help purchase returned or "odd lot" furnishings.

Supplies

Along with fixtures, decorations, and equipment, some of the following supplies may be needed to keep the retail space clean, attractive, and sanitary. If there is a storage room, consider keeping these supplies on hand to save the hassle of having to go to the store if supplies run out and to take advantage of bulk pricing through business supply stores.

For the showroom:

- ✓ Furniture polish
- ✓ Dust cloths
- ✓ Vacuum cleaner bags
- ✓ Disinfectant spray
- ✓ First aid kit
- ✓ Window cleaner
- ✓ Paper towels
- ✓ Air freshener
- ✓ Pens
- ✓ Candy or mints

For the bathroom:

- ✓ Hand soap
- ✓ Toilet paper
- ✓ Disinfectant spray
- ✓ Lotion
- ✓ Air freshener
- ✓ Paper towels

For the employee area:

- ✓ Hand sanitizer
- ✓ Paper towels
- ✓ Band aids

- ✓ Time cards
- ✓ Pens
- ✓ Notebooks

Behind the counter:

- ✓ Cash register tape
- ✓ Boxes
- ✓ Shopping bags

- ✓ Gift wrapping supplies
- ✓ Pens and pencils

For the office:

- ✓ Printer paper
- ✓ Toner
- ✓ Computer storage media (CDs, tapes, or disks)

- ✓ Coin wrappers
- ✓ Deposit tickets/ checks

Creating Ambience

The color palette, furnishings, and decorations help set the mood for customers, but they usually only stimulate two senses: sight and touch. To complete the ambience of the retail space, consider adding layers of sound and smell to the shopping experience.

Many stores play music in the background. This is an easy way to highlight the business's desired image. A highbrow furniture store might want classical music tickling through the displays. For a trendy boutique, the latest pop hits might be more suitable.

Music is not the only way to add a sound element to the store. Waterfalls, wind chimes, and white noise CDs can also be used effectively. When using sound in the store, remember that some people are bothered by constant or loud noises. Try to make the sounds barely noticeable, not overbearing.

For those who are going to play a CD, record, or tape in the store, permission will need to be obtained, as the music publisher, composer, or lyricist still owns the rights to any public performance. There are two licensing agencies in the United States, ASCAP and BMI. To make sure licensing regulations are being complied with, contact both agencies to obtain permission before playing any copyrighted music in the business.

CONTACT INFORMATION FOR MUSIC LICENSING AGENCIES	
BMI	212-586-2000
ASCAP	800-95-ASCAP or **www.ascap.com**

Fragrance can also help get customers in the mood to shop. Simmering potpourri, the smell of fresh linens, or a light spray of lavender are most commonly used, but other scents can be tried that may be more appropriate for the merchandise. For example, try pine or cinnamon for Christmas ornaments, or fresh cut citrus for bath products.

Large retailers often use different scents throughout the store, tailoring the fragrances for different displays. Like music, scents usually work best when they are subtle and barely noticeable.

Signs

Depending on the business and location, consider purchasing signs for the following locations:

- **Outside the store, on the building.**

- **In the front window:** A well-lit sign in the window can announce the business name or the details of current promotions.

- **Outside the store, in the parking area:** If the store is in a busy, high traffic area, a sign can help customers know they are at the right place.

- **Inside the store:** Signs inside the store can be used for decorative elements or to highlight certain products.

- **On the road (billboard):** If the store is off the beaten path or a product with wide appeal is offered, a billboard can help potential patrons find the store.

Amateurish signs tend to make establishments look tasteless, dated, and unprofessional. A professional printer and graphic designer can help create signs that will fit with the store's image.

Insurance

Before opening the store insurance will be needed to protect the inventory and equipment in case of damage, as well as liability insurance in case a customer or employee is injured on the premises. Home and rental insurance may not cover business related losses, so even if the business is being run online or as a catalog store, supplemental business insurance may be needed.

Depending on the type of retail store being established, the following may be needed:

- ✓ **Workers' compensation insurance** — which will cover the costs if one of the employees is hurt on the job.

- ✓ **Liability insurance** — which will pay if someone is hurt at the site.

- ✓ **Product liability** — in case someone is hurt using a product the store sells.

- ✓ **Vandalism insurance** — to cover losses from malicious acts.

- ✓ **Contents and personal property insurance** — a broad policy that usually covers the replacement cost of damaged goods.

- ✓ **Business operations insurance** — another broad policy which can be tailored to cover business documents, injuries, legal expenses, health care, and many other needs.

In addition, if the building in which the business will be operating is owned, the owner may want to consider insuring it against damage caused by:

- ✓ Fire

- ✓ Earthquake

- ✓ Floods

Laws, Regulations, and Licenses

Owners of a retail store will need to learn about the local, state, and federal laws that affect the business.

The forms that will have to be filed to keep the business compliant will vary according to what the business sells, where it operates, and how the store is structured. The local Clerk of Courts can help determine exactly what licenses and permits will be needed. These may include the following:

- ✓ **Business license**

- ✓ **Specialized retail licenses**

- ✓ **Building permit**

- ✓ **Fictitious name application** — also called a DBA or "Doing Business As."

- ✓ **Zoning permit**

- ✓ **Certificate of occupancy**

- ✓ **Tax registrations**

- ✓ **Health and safety permit**

- ✓ **Police permit**

- ✓ **Fire department permit**

- ✓ **Sign permit**

More information can be found out about pertinent requirements using the following resources:

✓ **The U.S. Business Resource Library (www.business.gov):** Managed by 22 government agencies, this site is the official business link to the U.S. government. Compliancy requirements, links to other resources, and online counseling can be found here.

✓ **Local Business Incubators:** Many universities offer aid and advising to small businesses through their business departments.

✓ **U.S. Department of Labor (www.dol.gov/elaws):** Businesses planning on hiring employees will have additional regulations to follow.

✓ **The state government Web site:** Many states have agencies dedicated to helping entrepreneurs navigate the legal aspects of business ownership.

While preparing to open a retail business, a rather hefty stack of paperwork may be collected, each seeming to ask for the same information. Filing for licenses and permits is not the most exciting or glamorous part of owning a retail business, but failing to complete all required state and local forms may result in large fines.

State Registration

Most states require new businesses to register before opening. The Secretary of State's office can help with the procedure by providing with the necessary forms for state registration. The name of the company may also need to be registered using a fictitious name or "doing business as" application.

If employees need to be hired, the state Department of Labor or Taxation can provide information to calculate how much state and local tax will need to be withheld.

Local Registration

The city and county may require a new business to apply for a business license. After applying, the local zoning board will review the business information to make sure it is in compliancy with local regulations.

Sales Tax

Most states, and many cities and counties, require taxes to be collected on every retail sale. In order to do this, a vendor's license must be held. In order to apply for a vendor's license, contact the state revenue or taxation agency. They can explain how to collect, report, and pay sales tax.

Fire Department Permit

When opening a traditional bricks-and-mortar store, contact the local fire department to learn about regulations and to schedule an inspection of the store. At the inspection, the fire official is likely to:

- ✓ Make sure fire exits are available.

- ✓ Check that smoke detectors are installed and working.

- ✓ Ensure that a fire extinguisher is on the premises.

- ✓ Establish a maximum capacity for the store.

- ✓ See that all regulations are being followed.

Sign Permit

Many neighborhoods limit the size, height, placement, style, and lighting of signs. The local government may require a permit before displaying a sign over a certain size. Be aware of and follow any local rules governing signs for the store.

Federal Identification Number

Unless the business is a sole proprietorship with no employees, the business will need to register for a Federal Identification Number (FIN), which will be used on the business's tax forms and license applications. To obtain an FIN, file IRS Form #SS-4, which is also on the accompanying CD. Make sure that you use the newest version of the form.

For those who are a sole proprietor without any employees, use a Social Security Number for any forms that require an FIN.

PUBLIC UTILITIES

Be sure to notify public utility companies well in advance. Some of the utilities that may be needed for a retail business include:

- ✓ **Telephone**
- ✓ **Gas**
- ✓ **Electric**
- ✓ **Water**

Many utility companies require a deposit before providing service. Make sure to check with service providers about their procedures.

13

ACCOUNTING AND BOOKKEEPING

THE IMPORTANCE OF KEEPING ACCURATE RECORDS

As a retail business grows and develops, owners may find themselves becoming swamped in records and numbers. Between invoices, receipts, paychecks, loan payments, and tax returns, it is easy to lose track of expenses and incomes.

Using a reliable bookkeeping system will help keep these records in order and be more aware of the financial situation of the business.

Legal

It is a legal obligation to keep good records of business transactions. In order to file accurate tax returns, it is important to know business expenses, income, and credit. If the business is audited, the reported calculations may need to be proved valid.

In addition, the IRS requires that business records and employment tax records are kept for specific periods of time, the length of which is determined by the type of record, the action taken with regards to the record, and the expense recorded. For more information on document storage requirements, contact the IRS or visit **www.irs.gov**.

Financial

Beyond the legal necessity, good bookkeeping makes financial sense. Being able to review what money is coming in and what money is leaving the business will help determine the store's financial well-being. This will also put the business in a better position to see where it has the opportunity to economize.

Marketing

To many business owners, good accounting practices feed directly into their marketing efforts. Tracking the flow of money throughout the month will help determine what advertising campaigns are working and what products are moving. Being able to review what inventory is sold when can help locate hot selling times, pinpoint effective price points, and learn more about the target market.

WHO SHOULD KEEP THE BOOKS?

When developing a bookkeeping system, the owner should either plan to hire someone to keep the records or do the task himself or herself.

Many bookkeepers work on a freelance basis, but even if a business is planning on hiring a bookkeeper, it is important to understand enough to notice problems and discrepancies. For those without any bookkeeping experience, the local college may offer courses to teach the necessary skills.

WHAT RECORDS ARE IMPORTANT?

The bookkeeping system should be able to handle the following types of documents:

Purchases: Items, including materials and parts, bought to resell to customers. Purchases are recorded using:

- ✓ Invoices
- ✓ Cash register tapes
- ✓ Cancelled checks
- ✓ Credit card charge slips

Receipts: Money that comes into the business. Receipts can be proven by:

- ✓ Credit card receipts
- ✓ Invoices
- ✓ Bank deposit slips

Expenses: Any costs to the business, excluding purchases. There are three basic types of business expenses. **Direct expenses** are those that are spent completely on the business; for example decorations, business loan interest, and office supplies. **Capital expenses** are more expensive items that benefit the retail business over a longer period of time. When filing taxes, the costs of capital expenses are extended over a period of time and depreciation is calculated. The IRS or a tax consultant can help calculate capital expenses. **Prorated expenses** are related to the mortgage interest and property tax if the business is being run from home. Expenses may be found on:

- ✓ Petty cash slips
- ✓ Cancelled checks
- ✓ Invoices
- ✓ Cash register tapes
- ✓ Account statements
- ✓ Credit card charge slips

Assets: Property that is owned and used for the business. Information about assets can be obtained from:

- ✓ Receipts
- ✓ Insurance statements
- ✓ Repair records
- ✓ Estimates
- ✓ Receipts

ACCOUNTING SOFTWARE

Programs like Peachtree (**www.peachtree.com**) and QuickBooks® (**www.quickbooks.com**) make routine bookkeeping tasks simpler and reduce arithmetic errors.

For smaller retail operations, Microsoft® (**www.microsoft.com**) offers a basic accounting program, *Office Accounting Express*, for free. The free version contains only rudimentary functions such as customer and vendor records, payments received, and refunds. However, there are many add-ons available, allowing only the needed features to be bought. With the ability to synchronize with eBay and PayPal, *Office Accounting Express* is especially suited for owners of small online stores. *Office Accounting Express* can be downloaded at **http://www.microsoft.com/smallbusiness/**.

Both Peachtree and QuickBooks® offer software packages bundled with different features. Simple versions can be bought that track sales and expenses or more pricey programs are available that handle payroll, point of sale, credit card processing, invoices, customer and vendor contact information, and cost analyses. The best software package is the one that meets a business's needs now and in the foreseeable future.

PAYROLL

If there will be employees at the retail store, it is very important to keep accurate payroll records. If there will be temporary or hourly employees, a time clock may be needed to keep track of the times each employee worked.

Most commercial bookkeeping software packages include modules to help process payrolls, but an accountant or payroll service may also be used.

A business will most likely want to calculate the payroll daily so that the costs and identify problems can easily be monitored. The bookkeeper may follow these steps when calculating payroll:

- ✓ Gather time cards.

- ✓ Verify the information on the time cards. If any employees clocked in early, check with the manager to make sure they were working and needed.

- ✓ Calculate the hours for each employee.

- ✓ Enter the hours on the payroll form or time cards, highlighting overtime hours.

✓   Look up the hourly wage for each employee.

✓   Multiply hours worked by appropriate hourly wage to determine daily gross pay.

✓   Prorate salaried employees' yearly income for one day.

✓   Add all gross pays for the day. This is the *total daily gross pay.*

✓   At the end of the week, total each employee's daily gross pay to yield his or her weekly gross pay.

✓   Double check calculations by comparing the sums of the total daily gross pays for the week with the sum of all employees' weekly gross pays. The numbers should be equal.

✓   Complete a Labor Analysis Form using daily sales and gross pays.

Keeping a close eye on labor costs can help decide when new employees need to be added and when hours might need to be scaled back.

In addition to calculating gross wages, each payday that is to be withheld, deposit and report certain employment taxes from the employees' paychecks. Responsibilities include:

✓   Withholding federal income tax.

✓   Withholding Social Security and Medicare taxes.

✓   Paying advance earned income credit payment if requested.

✓   Depositing withheld taxes.

TAXES

Tax season can be a very confusing time for retail business owners. Luckily, the latest generation of tax preparation software takes away most of the potential for mathematical errors on returns. These programs are only as reliable as the information that is fed to them, however. An accountant or tax professional can help a business understand what tax laws apply to it.

If a retail business is a sole proprietorship with no employees, the business income and expenses may be filed along with personal taxes. If a business is a corporation or partnership, or if there are some workers on your payroll, separate taxes will need to be filed under the Federal Identification Number or Employee Identification Number.

If there are employees, the owner will have quarterly and annual tax reporting responsibilities regarding withheld income tax, Social Security and Medicare taxes, and Federal unemployment (FUTA) taxes.

For more information about tax laws and requirements, visit the IRS at **www.irs.gov**. Some of the forms and publications that should be downloaded are:

- ✓ Publication 15, Employer's Tax Guide

- ✓ Form 940 (or 940-EZ), Employer's Annual Federal Unemployment (FUTR) Tax Return

- ✓ Form 941, Employer's Quarterly Federal Tax Return

Form 940 is due by January 31 each year. Form 941 is due one month after the calendar month or quarter ends, as determined by the amount of payment. These forms are available on the accompanying CD.

HANDLING TRANSACTIONS

Retail store owners will want to make sales. Often a good product and competitive pricing are not enough. Making it easy for a customer to buy from a business is important, or else they are likely to find somewhere else to spend their money.

One way to encourage patrons to purchase goods is to allow them to pay using their choice of a variety of methods. At the very least, accept the following types of payment:

- ✓ Cash

- ✓ Personal checks

- ✓ Credit cards

- ✓ Debit cards

In addition, consider accepting some of the following payment options:

- ✓ Store credit account

- ✓ Business checks

- ✓ Store gift cards

- ✓ Discount coupons

- ✓ Store vouchers for returned merchandise

- ✓ Community scrip

The bookkeeping system should be equipped to keep track of transactions made with all the payment methods accepted.

Be sure to incorporate policies to help protect the business from fraudulent transactions. For example:

- ✓ To reduce losses due to accepting counterfeit bills, train employees to spot fakes and have a strict protocol for handling suspect money. A bank can help a business learn to identify fake bills. Counterfeit detector pens are also available.

- ✓ If checks are accepted, consider using a check verification service such as TeleCheck®, Certegy®, SCAN, or Verified. Some cities require businesses to use check confirmation systems.

- ✓ Write the customer's telephone number on his or her check. This will make it easier to contact the customer if there is a problem.

- ✓ Most retail businesses do not accept third party, starter, or counter checks.

✓   Customers should show identification and sign the front of travelers' checks.

✓   Institute and enforce a return check policy.

✓   Ask for photo identification to help verify credit card and debit card ownership.

✓   In order to track store vouchers and gift certificates, print them with consecutive numbers.

✓   After the sale, file any used gift certificates, store vouchers, or coupons in a designated envelope so they can be used when reconciling the daily ledger.

In order to file accurate taxes and to make better decisions about labor, inventory, and marketing, it is imperative to keep accurate records of every sale.

One way to keep better track of retail transactions is to assign each cashier a separate cash register drawer. The owner, or the shift manager, should have each cash drawer prepared and assigned. At the start of a shift, have the cashier recount the drawer and sign a receipt verifying the amount.

During a shift, only the manager and the assigned cashier should have access to the register drawer. At the end of each shift, the cashier should count the drawer and use the register report to balance the totals.

If the money in a drawer does not agree with the register report, the owner or the shift manager needs to double check the amounts, write up the discrepancy, and sign the report.

At the end of the day, checks and credit card receipts should be totaled and stored in the safe until they can be deposited. Cash should be tallied separately.

14

BUDGETING AND OPERATIONAL MANAGEMENT

An important way to evaluate how a retail business is performing is to analyze the *cash flow*. The cash flow measures all the money coming into and being paid out by the company.

A *budget* is the planned cash flow. Setting a budget and routinely comparing the estimated revenue and expenses to the actual cash flow will help make realistic long-term financial projections. Whenever there is a discrepancy, try to find the cause and implement a solution as soon as possible.

When a retail business's monthly and yearly cash flow can be predicted, a business may be able better able to use its working budget to achieve the following goals:

- ✓ Take advantage of lower rates and favorable terms by paying suppliers early.

- ✓ Save for large equipment or real estate purchases.

- ✓ Hold reserves to maintain cash flow during slow sales periods.

- ✓ Determine if a business loan is needed and can be paid back.

- ✓ Convince potential financers of the business's fiscal health.

- ✓ Take advantage of bulk sales for inventory or supplies.

OPERATIONAL EXPENSES

In accounting terminology, *purchases* are expenses related to the products being retailed. They may include inventory or materials used to produce the inventory. *Operational expenses*, on the other hand, include any money that is paid out related to the day-to-day running of the business. Operational expenses do not include purchases.

Another way of looking at operational expenses is to consider it the money used to make the inventory become income. The operational expenses may include:

✓ Labor	✓ Supplies
✓ Utilities	✓ Rent
✓ Marketing	✓ Services
✓ Depreciation	

Labor

Depending on how the business is structured, labor may be one of the largest operational expenses. If the business is a sole proprietorship with no employees, labor may not be a concern at all.

If there are employees, there are three types of labor expenses that may apply to the operation: fixed monthly salaries, hourly wages, and overtime.

Fixed Monthly Salaries

Managers and owners will most likely be paid fixed monthly salaries, despite the number of hours worked. To determine a salaried employee's exact cost for a given month, divide the yearly salary by the number of days in the year, then multiply by the number of days in the month. Be sure to update the budget to reflect bonuses and raises.

Hourly Wages

These are salaries that fluctuate based on the number of hours each employee works. Of course, employee work schedules are based on the store need, which in turn is based on how much inventory is sold. For this reason, it is important to constantly evaluate how much is being paid out in labor costs throughout the day, week, and month as compared to the sales volume. The goal should be to find a point where manpower costs are minimized without hurting the profit or customer service.

Overtime

According to the Fair Labor Standards Act (FLSA), overtime is defined as any time worked over 40 hours per week. FLSA states that employees must be paid for overtime hours at a rate of at least 150 percent their usual hourly wage. Many states and cities have additional overtime regulations.

Because it is so expensive, overtime should be avoided. During the holiday sales season, many retailers find that overtime is inevitable. If this is the case, try to keep it at a minimum. Consider hiring seasonal or temporary help or using creative scheduling to avoid having to pay overtime.

The most thoughtfully arranged schedule can be thwarted if employees do not follow it. A policy requiring prior approval before switching shifts can help reduce overtime payout. Be sure to carefully tally employee's hours before agreeing to any schedule changes.

Supplies

Supplies include any non-inventory goods that have to be replaced frequently. As the business's operations are fine tuned, a better idea will be formed as to what supplies need to be bought and how frequently they will be purchased.

Supplies may include:

✓ Printer paper and toner

✓ Cleaning supplies

- ✓ Disposable paper goods

- ✓ Pens and pencils

- ✓ Computer CDs to back up financial information

- ✓ Deposit tickets and checks

Consumable supplies can be a large chunk of the budget, but there are ways to reduce the cost. Large office supply stores and business-to-business discount warehouses are often great places to find computer, cleaning, and paper goods — especially when buying in bulk. However, it is easy to get overwhelmed by the variety of goods available at these stores. Going armed with a shopping list and budget can help a person resist the urge to buy supplies that are not needed or a higher quality that really cannot be afforded.

Many office supply stores have Web sites. If there is a free membership program for businesses, consider joining. There may be valuable perks such as free shipping and special pricing.

Other Expenses

There may be several other expenses that affect the budget. Some may be steady from month to month while the cost of others may vary widely depending on how much is sold, the time of the year, employee turnover, and many other factors.

Services

As a retail business is started, the owner may need to consult with an accountant, a lawyer, and a marketing advisor. As the business grows, it may be necessary to work with these professionals more. Consider preparing for this by setting aside a little money every month toward future consulting expenses.

There may also be some ongoing service costs, including security, freight, and maintenance. Security costs may be the same each month unless systems or providers are changed. Freight costs, on the other hand, can change each month in response to fuel costs, labor issues, and how many deliveries are required.

Owners might be tempted to save money by performing routine maintenance as infrequently as possible. Unfortunately, this is a plan that tends to backfire. Failing to perform timely maintenance of building or business equipment can lead to expensive repairs or replacements. Not keeping the parking lot, windows, and walkways clean, free of snow, and in good condition can hurt the business's image and possibly lead to liability issues.

Training

Business owners are responsible for ensuring that employees are able to safely operate equipment, correctly use appropriate computer programs, and understand the products being sold. This may require training the employees at the store or sending them to a training facility.

Most employee training happens "on the clock," which means a business is expected to pay employees that are learning and not yet productive. One way to reduce training costs is to provide a friendly work atmosphere in order to keep employee turnover rates low.

Depreciation

Capital assets are those expenses that are useful for more than one year. Some common capital expenses that might be purchased for a retail business include vehicles, cash registers, computers, display cases, and safes.

Depreciation reflects the change of value due to "wear and tear" on an asset. A car with 60,000 miles on it, for example, is not worth as much as it was when it was new.

Because a capital asset is used over a longer period, the tax deductible depreciation costs must be spread over the asset's usable life. The IRS has established guidelines for determining a capital asset's usable life. An accountant can help explain the depreciation rules that apply to a business and its assets.

Marketing

There may be ongoing marketing expenses associated with a business. Depending on the marketing strategy, these costs may be constant or may change every month. If a marketing blast is planned around a holiday, sale, or event, be sure to budget for it throughout the year.

The marketing budget may include the costs of:

- ✓ Billboards

- ✓ Newspaper advertisements

- ✓ Radio/television commercials

- ✓ Brochures and pamphlets

- ✓ Web site development

- ✓ Direct mailings

- ✓ Online advertisements

- ✓ Sponsoring sporting events

- ✓ Promotional items

Charitable Contributions

As the business grows, consider donating some of the profits to charitable organizations. These contributions can help promote the business, enhance its image, and improve the community.

Utilities

Depending on where the retail business is established, some of the following utilities may need to be included in the budget:

✓ **Telephone:** Even when running a business from home, a designated phone line or upgraded service package may be needed. Telephone costs should be fairly constant, especially if a usage policy is instituted. If there are unexplained telephone expenses, compare the numbers listed on the phone bill to the work schedule to help identify the cause.

✓ **Water:** For most retail businesses, there should not be much variation in the water bill. If the service provider charges quarterly or if the business has a seasonal need for water, consider budgeting for the water bill throughout the year.

✓ **Gas:** If the store is heated with gas, there might be a widely fluctuating bill throughout the year. The gas company may be able to devise a budget payment plan to help a business pay a more consistent amount every month.

✓ **Electricity:** Like gas, electricity costs often cycle throughout the year. If the service provider does not have a budget plan, consider setting extra aside for future electricity costs each month.

✓ **Internet service:** If the retail business model includes an online store, reliable Web and e-mail hosting will be needed. This will likely be a constant expense every month.

Rent

Budgeting is easier if the lease agreement sets a specific monthly cost to rent the store or equipment. If the rent is based on the sales or profit, be sure to budget a realistic amount. Sometimes landlords will offer a reduced rental arrangement for the first few months, to allow the business to become established. If that is the case, be certain to update the budget numbers to reflect the change in cost after the honeymoon period.

Taxes

The owner will be responsible for withholding and paying labor and sales taxes. In addition, the budget should anticipate any property, state, local, and federal taxes.

Insurance

Most insurance agencies can arrange monthly, quarterly, or yearly insurance premiums.

Repairs

Being prepared for equipment or building repairs can keep an inconvenience from becoming a financial emergency. Be aware of potential problems and budget money for repairs.

Shipping/Postage

If a business ships merchandise or mails catalogs, post cards, or flyers, a good chunk of the budget may be spent at the post office or delivery service. To help save on costs, try to keep packages in standard size boxes. The United States Postal Service and other shipping services offer customers free packing materials when specific services are used. In addition, bulk mailings may qualify for special postage rates, as do books and other bound, printed material. The following Web sites can provide more information about ways to save on business shipping and postage needs:

- ✓   The United States Postal Service (**www.usps.com/business**)

- ✓   FedEx (**www.mysmallbizcenter.com**)

- ✓   UPS (**www.ups.com/content/us/en/bussol/smallbiz/index. html?WT.svl=SubNav**)

Travel

Retail business owners may need to travel to many places, including:

- ✓   Trade shows

✓   Franchise training programs

✓   Supplier warehouses or factories

✓   Industry conventions

✓   Meetings with potential investors

✓   Employee training retreats

These trips may be known about well in advance, allowing the business to budget for them.

Loan Repayment/Credit Card Bills

If a business has loan or credit card payments, be sure to include them in the budget. Some loan interest may be tax deductible.

Trade Association Dues

Joining associations and organizations related to the merchandise being sold can be an effective way of letting potential customers know about a business. It may also be beneficial to join a retailer association or the Better Business Bureau. Most associations charge yearly dues, so divide the cost by 12 to budget for them monthly.

Licenses

A business may need to budget for recurring licensing fees. In addition to the business license, if certain products are retailed, such as food or alcohol, additional licenses may need to be obtained.

Bad Debt

Bad debt expenses are those that are incurred from bounced checks or fraudulent credit card transactions. If the business is unable to collect on these debts, the full amount is tax deductible.

REVENUE

In addition to expenses, the budget should include realistic income estimates. Later, be sure to compare the budget numbers with the actual cash flow.

Retail Sales

When running a retail business, most of the income likely comes from retail sales. By keeping track of the models and styles of merchandise being sold, how they were displayed, any advertising tools that were used, the final selling price, and how the sale was conducted, valuable information will be gained to help with future pricing, stocking, and marketing decisions.

Depending on the business model, consider making retail sales to customers in person, online, or through catalogs.

In Person

In person transactions can be made in the store, through door-to-door contact, at sales shows, or any other retail situation in which a salesperson is in personal contact with the customer.

Online

Online sales occur when a customer selects and pays for merchandise through a Web site. Online sales generally have less overhead than in person sales, as an employee or physical store does not need to be available in order to help the customer. Since the Web site will be available 24 hours a day, customers can shop at their leisure.

Catalog

Catalog sales occur when a customer selects merchandise through a physical or online catalog, then telephones, visits, or e-mails the business to place the order. Many MLM businesses rely on catalog sales.

Other Revenue Sources

Just because a business is a retail store does not mean its only stream of revenue needs to be retail sales. Diversifying income opportunities may have several benefits, including:

✓ **Better serving the target market.** If there is a population of people interested in the products being sold, they may be interested in services surrounding those products. Customers who purchase beads and jewelry fastenings, for instance, may also be interested in jewelry making classes.

✓ **Encourage repeat customers.** A customer who pays a nominal amount to join a purchasing program may visit the store again later to take further advantage of the discounted prices.

✓ **Providing income through sales slumps.** If it is found that sales are cyclical, scheduling classes or providing extra services during the down times may help the net profit.

✓ **Establishing authority.** The more high quality peripheral services that are offered, the better the business will be able to place itself as an expert in the field, and differentiate itself from any competitors. There may be many shoe stores in the area, but one could be the only one that offers shoe repairs and expert fitting.

✓ **Increased retail sales.** If classes are offered, require students to buy their materials through the store, or offer discounts on future purchases.

Classes

Hosting educational events can separate a business from competitors, especially chain stores. If a store can position itself as a place to come for information, not just materials, more of the target market may choose to shop at the store.

If the inventory is related to a hobby, lifestyle, or special interest, consider offering classes. If a health supply store is owned, customers may be interested in nutrition or alternative medicine classes. If an antiques store is owned, consider holding a class on the different historic styles of furniture. Consider inviting experts in to give lectures or workshops.

"How-to" classes can be quite profitable, especially if special kits with all the materials students need to complete a successful project are packaged and sold. If an auto parts store is owned, how about a class on changing oil with a kit including an oil pan, funnel, oil filter wrench, oil filter, gloves, and oil?

Purchasing Programs

Purchasing programs allow customers to get discount prices or special services for an upfront fee. An office supply store, for instance, may offer cards that allow customers a free box of copy paper for every $50 purchase. A bookstore may give card holders a 20 percent discount on all purchases.

Purchasing programs encourage customer loyalty. The key is to keep the price low enough and the benefits high enough to entice people to pay for membership.

There are several different types of purchasing program benefits that can be offered to customers, including:

- ✓ **Discount on every purchase:** Members receive a specified percent off everything they buy.

- ✓ **Free shipping/delivery:** The business pays all shipping fees for members' purchases.

- ✓ **Exclusive offers:** Members get the first look at new merchandise, can register for classes early, or get to attend sales before the store officially opens.

- ✓ **Buy something, get something:** Members receive free or discounted goods and services with a certain number of purchases.

✓ **Referral bonus:** Members receive store credit or discounts for referring new customers.

✓ **Points:** Members earn points, which they can later redeem for goods or services, based on their purchases.

Services

Customers may need someone to help them install, learn to use, or even choose their merchandise. Consider offering services related to the products for a small fee. If a toy store is owned, for instance, put together bicycles. If a computer store is owned, install software or offer a backup service. If a clothing store is owned, provide alterations and hemming.

Warranties

If high-ticket items that may require expensive maintenance are sold, warranties or extended service policies may give customers peace of mind. Be sure to check with the manufacturer to make sure any plans being offered do not interfere with their guarantees.

Wholesaling

If a business finds itself with large amounts of slow moving products, consider selling the excessive inventory at wholesale rates to another business. Another store may cater to a market better suited to those items and storage and shelf space will be freed up for faster moving products. Make sure that wholesale reselling does not violate any licensing agreement or exclusivity deal with the supplier.

Business-to-Business Sales

Other businesses may need the items being sold. They may require them to decorate their offices, to help their business run, or to give away as Christmas gifts.

TOTAL NET PROFIT

The net profit or loss is calculated by subtracting the total expenses from the total revenue.

MONTHLY BUDGETING

As an owner gains more experience operating a retail business, he or she may find it easier to create a realistic monthly budget. It is usually a good idea to spread the cost of pricey, infrequent expenses over several months to try to keep the cash flow closer to constant from month to month.

ANALYZING AND USING THE NUMBERS

If a business has been consistent about writing monthly budgets and comparing them to actual expenses and revenue, it will have a growing set of data about the business's performance, labor effectiveness, and growth.

Tracking Sales Trends

If a business has kept good records of what inventory was purchased and what has sold, patterns can be identified that can help with marketing and displaying and pricing the merchandise.

On a weekly or monthly basis, use the revenue and expense data to answer the following useful questions:

- ✓ **Turnaround:** Which products sat on the shelves the least amount of time? How were they displayed? How were they priced? What related items did customers purchase?

- ✓ **Marketing:** What advertising campaigns were particularly useful? Was there a spike in sales after certain television, radio, or newspaper spots?

- ✓ **Future Purchases:** Are any products being sold that have accessories that are not currently in stock? Can any slow moving products be bundled with fast sellers?

✓ **Pricing:** Are products selling well at the current price? Would they sell as well if they were priced higher? Can the price be cut on any slow-moving products?

Calculating Sales Growth

Recording the net profit of the business is one way to determine the sales growth. Another is by tracking unit profit margins. The profit margin is calculated by subtracting the total expense of offering the product from the purchase price.

It is usually better for the bottom line to sell fewer high margin items than many low margin items, but that is not always the case. Be looking for possible ways of increasing the margin on the different types of products being retailed. Some ways of doing this include:

✓ Raising the retail price.

✓ Bundling high margin items with low margin items; for example, a high margin warranty policy with a low margin appliance.

✓ Bundling several related low margin products together.

Cutting Costs

After analyzing the cash flow, the fact that more money is going out of the business than coming in may be realized. This is where the budget will come in handy. Compare the estimated expenditures to the actual costs and ask the following questions:

✓ Where has more been spent than budgeted?

✓ Was overspending due to an unexpected event? If more was spent on supplies to take advantage of bulk prices, for example, the cost may be made up with future savings in that category.

✓   Will the business be able to stay within budget in the future?

✓   If the income was smaller than expected, can more money be transferred into marketing?

✓   Are there any areas where spending can be cut without hurting quality or customer service?

Predicting Future Trends

One of the most useful benefits of maintaining accurate sales records is the ability to better predict future business ebbs and flows. Most retail stores experience cyclical sales. Knowing about the periodic slow periods can help business owners create better budgets. They will be able to hold some money back during high profit times to help with cash flow when there is not much revenue.

Depending on what merchandise they offer, they may sell more during certain seasons. A garden supply center, for instance, may do much brisker business in the spring and summer. A jewelry store may have peaks during the Christmas season and right before Valentine's Day.

Other fluctuations might not be so obvious. A coffee store near an elementary school might be packed with moms during the half hour or so before the bell rings, but empty during the summer. In this situation, the owner can use some creative methods to bring in customers during the slow times. For instance, he or she can schedule children's programs during the summer to help draw mothers back to the shop or offer an "early bird special" before noon.

Being able to forecast sales slumps will help create better budgets and plan alternate streams of revenue or marketing approaches.

15

USING TECHNOLOGY

Technology has affected nearly every part of life: communication, research, shopping, and running a business.

Used correctly, a computer can help analyze finances, organize inventory, make transactions easier, and reach more potential customers. If the cheapest software and the first system that comes along are purchased, however, money may be wasted, putting the business and personal information at risk, and frustrating employees and customers.

YOUR BUSINESS WEB SITE AND E-MAIL

A company Web site is not necessary to run a successful retail business. Having one, however, can be very beneficial. A well-designed Web site can:

✓ **Enhance a business's image.** If a customer cannot find the store on the Internet, the business may look behind the times.

✓ **Increase sales.** Adding an online store to a business model can help distant customers purchase the products.

✓ **Improve communication.** Updating the Web site is cheaper and easier than sending out multiple bulk mailings. With a Web site, customers can see new products quickly and get in touch about any questions.

SECURING A DOMAIN NAME

To create an online presence for a business, first choose a domain name registrar and a Web site hosting service. Often, hosting services will also handling registering a domain name, but it can be cheaper to do these steps with different companies.

Through a domain name registrar, a domain name can be registered with the International Corporation for Assigned Names and Numbers ICANN). A domain name is the host name for e-mail or a Web site. Domain names are usually only letters and numbers followed by ".com, ".org," ".biz," or another extension. A list of ICANN accredited registrars can be found at **http://www.icann.org/registrars/accredited-list.html**.

After choosing a domain name registrar, a domain name must be chosen. Most registrars will be able to tell immediately if a name is available for purchase.

Choosing a domain name is not a task to be taken lightly. The Web site and e-mail addresses will be on stationery and advertisements. The perfect domain name should be:

- ✓ **Simple:** The fewer words the better.

- ✓ **Memorable:** Customers should be able to visit the Web site even if they have lost the business card.

- ✓ **Unique:** If the domain name is close to a competitor's, visitors might wander there by mistake.

- ✓ **Applicable:** A good domain name should include the business's name or what is sold.

Because so many domain names are already taken, it is a good idea to have several choices ready. If possible, try to purchase the .com extension. Consider buying the .net, .org, and .biz variations of the domain name, if they are available. That way, they will not be used by a competing store.

Choose a Web site hosting service, which will save the Web site on their server and allow people to view it over the Internet. There are many types of hosting services available. Some questions to answer when researching service providers include:

✓ How much will the service cost every month?

✓ What are the upfront costs?

✓ Is there a plan to meet the size and complexity of a Web site?

✓ How reliable is the service?

✓ How often does the host experience service downtime (try to find one that guarantees less than one percent downtime)?

✓ How long has the service been in business?

✓ Is there any special e-commerce software, such as shopping carts and checkout utilities, available through the host?

✓ How secure is the hosting service?

✓ Is e-mail hosting available?

✓ What kinds of technical support are offered?

✓ Is there an extra fee for technical support?

✓ If a business Web site needs to increase, can a more appropriate plan be switched to?

✓ If a business chooses to change service providers, how hard will it be to transfer the Web site?

✓ Does the host provide any software to help build a Web site or upload it to their servers?

✓ What type of reputation does the service provider have?

✓ What extensions (Perl, JavaScript™, Flash, etc.) does the hosting service support?

✓ How fast are the servers?

✓ How much space is given?

✓ Does the host provide any data backup services?

✓　What types of logging and analysis software is available?

✓　How long of a service contract will have to be signed?

An e-mail host will also be needed. Most business Web site hosting packages include e-mail hosting. However, those wanting a separate e-mail host will have plenty to choose from. Some companies offer free e-mail services, but these usually tack advertisements at the end of e-mail messages, have limited storage capabilities, and may be unreliable.

Whether looking for a separate e-mail host or hoping to bundle e-mail needs with the Web site hosting package, consider the following questions:

✓　How many e-mail aliases will be given?

✓　Is there Web-based access?

✓　Are there any file exchange restrictions?

✓　How reliable is the e-mail service?

✓　How much technical support is available?

✓　How much storage space is available per e-mail address?

✓　How difficult is it to change service providers?

There are many low cost options in Web site and e-mail hosting. With some research, a reliable, affordable package can be found that can meet and grow with the business's needs.

CREATING A WEB SITE

The Web site reflects the company's image. It is a combination of a catalog, a business card, and a billboard. What is included and how it is presented will help brand a business. A good, thoughtfully designed Web site can help attract the target market. A poor design will have visitors clicking to the competition.

What to Include

Before creating a Web site, have an idea of the information that should be contained. Will it be a stand alone retail experience, where visitors can purchase inventory? Will it only be an online advertisement for the brick-and-mortar store? Is it a source of information for the target market about the kind of products being sold?

The purpose of the Web site will determine which of the following features are included.

Catalog

An online catalog is a list of the merchandise the retail store carries. Consider including prices, specifications, and pictures. It is important to organize the Web site catalog so that visitors can find the products they are looking for. A search application can make using the catalog easier for potential customers.

Shopping Cart

For customers to be able to order merchandise directly from the online catalog, a shopping cart and checkout application will need to be included.

Contact Information

If customers will need to call or e-mail a business to purchase items, it is essential that contact information is easy to find. Put it on every page of the Web site, on a separate page, or both. Even if online purchases are allowed, be sure to make the telephone number, e-mail address, and mailing address easy to find in case customers have questions or problems.

About

If there is an interesting story about how the business started or if there are some special credentials regarding the merchandise, tell customers about it. If there is a brick-and-mortar store, consider a page detailing the hours of operation and location. Include directions to the store and local places of interest.

Policies

The Web site is a great place to post the business's policies about returns, returned checks, price matching, and coupons.

Employment

If the business regularly looks for employees, consider a job listing page on the Web site.

Blog

Blogging, or journaling, about the business can be a great way to bring visitors to the site and keep them coming back. To make the blog an asset to the Web site, follow these guidelines:

- ✓ Keep it relevant
- ✓ Keep it interesting
- ✓ Keep it updated

Some topics to consider discussing in a blog include:

- ✓ The pros and cons of business ownership.
- ✓ New inventory being offered.
- ✓ Reviews of merchandise.
- ✓ Attractions and events near the store.
- ✓ New regulations that will impact the business or target market.
- ✓ Ways customers can enjoy the products.
- ✓ Interviews with suppliers.
- ✓ Upcoming events that may interest the target market.

✓　　Reviews of trade shows and association meetings.

It is easy to let the blog collect figurative dust at the corner of the Web site or become a sounding board for complaints about customers, competitors, suppliers, and employees. Try to keep the blog positive and make it an enjoyable read. The goal should be to keep potential customers coming back to the site.

There are many free or low cost blogging software choices available. The Web site hosting service may even provide a version of *WordPress*, *MoveableType*, or another blogging program.

Coupons

Having coupons that shoppers can print out may encourage them to visit the store.

Calendar

If there are several events that relate to the inventory and would interest the target market, consider publishing an online calendar. This is also a good idea if the store offers classes, workshops, guest speakers, meetings, or regular sales.

Discussion Board

Serious hobbyists love to discuss their passions with people that share them. If a business usually sells to a niche market – whether it is field hockey players, Appalachian musicians, attachment parenting advocates, or women with curly hair – consider giving visitors a place to discuss the trends, tools, accessories, and techniques related to their pastime.

Music

Some new Web masters think that filling their Web sites with music will help them stand out from the competition. In reality, many Internet users find unexpected noises blaring at them an inconvenience. They are likely to close the page before they even get a chance to review the merchandise.

For those who think they need to have music on the retail business Web site, let it be the viewers' choice whether or not to listen to it. For example, if there is a clip from a CD being sold or an example of how an instrument sounds, offer the Web site visitor a button to push in order to hear the noise.

Online Sales Considerations

Giving visitors the chance to buy merchandise from the Web site can help expand a retail business's revenue. If a bricks-and-mortar shop is also operated, think about how to integrate these two sales streams. Some issues to address include:

✓   Will the same inventory be offered on the Web site as is available on the sales floor?

✓   Will there be different return policies based on how customers bought the merchandise?

✓   Will special sales be offered either online or in the store?

✓   Who will be responsible for keeping track of and shipping out online orders?

✓   How will the different types of sales be differentiated in the bookkeeping system?

Updates

The Web site will be a better sales and marketing tool if it is kept up-to-date. Customers will be frustrated if they visit the store to make a purchase based on the online catalog, only to find that the merchandise hasn't been carried in months. Online shoppers will be irritated if, after making a purchase, they receive an e-mail telling them that the product is no longer available.

Schedule time daily to review and revise the Web site to help ensure that it gives visitors the most accurate information about policies and available inventory.

Use a Professional or Build it Yourself?

It may be tempting to build and maintain a retail business Web site, but if the results are amateurish they may cost money in lost sales.

There are many WYSIWYG ("what you see is what you get") Web site editors, complete with templates, to help people get started creating a Web site. On the other hand, a professional designer can create a unique look for a site that will reflect the business image.

Before deciding to forgo a professional, ask the following questions:

✓   Are you familiar with computers and able to pick up programs quickly?

✓   Do you have a feel for what works and what does not in Web sites?

✓   Is there enough time to commit to creating and maintaining a Web site?

✓   Are you familiar with Web design standards?

✓   Is a modest looking Web site acceptable or is something splashier desired?

✓   Is there someone to bounce ideas off of and to contact when there are questions about designing the site?

✓   Is there enough money to invest in the necessary hardware (a good digital camera and scanner, for instance) and software?

When deciding to use a professional Web site designer, shop around. Different designers have different styles. Consider the following before contracting a designer:

✓   Is their portfolio appealing?

✓   Are they willing to work with a business if their submission is not exactly what is being sought?

✓ Do they have references? Do the references check out?

✓ Are they upfront about what will be provided? How many pages? Are pictures included? A checkout system?

✓ Will they upload the site onto the Web hosting server?

✓ Will they handle upgrades? If not, will they provide enough information for the business to upgrade the site?

✓ What kind of security features will they add to the Web site?

✓ Will they guarantee not to use the same design for another site?

✓ Have they designed Web sites for other retail businesses?

There are many Web site designers eager to work with small businesses. Electronic communication makes it possible to work with a designer on the other side of the world. As with any service, be sure of what you will be receiving and carefully read any agreements.

POINT OF SALE SYSTEMS

Modern cash registers can do so much more than just add up a list of prices. Point of sale (POS) systems can process credit card transactions, track employee performance, manage inventory, and exchange data with accounting software.

The POS software that is chosen will depend on what is being sold, what features are needed, and how much can be afforded.

Benefits of POS

A POS system can be a major business investment. Although a small or completely online business can be run without one, there are many ways that a good program can make life easier and a business more profitable:

✓ **Improved margins:** The detailed reports generated by a POS system can help analyze the margins on items and make more informed decisions about what inventory to push.

✓ **Less shrinkage:** *Shrinkage* is the loss of inventory due to shoplifting or waste. In many types of stores, employees are a major cause of shrinkage. If employees know that the inventory is being carefully monitored, they may be less apt to take, waste, or misuse merchandise.

✓ **Less paperwork:** Most POS systems automate repetitive chores.

✓ **Fewer transaction errors:** A POS system can make it easy to look up prices and calculate discounts and taxes.

✓ **Improved marketing capability:** By integrating a customer database with a POS system, contact information can be collected from shoppers. This will help build a mailing list of repeat customers.

Specialized Systems

There are many POS packages that have been written for specific types of retail stores. If a store sells automotive equipment, beauty supplies, apparel, CDs, books, gifts, toys, or other common inventories, the right software may be available.

Using prepackaged specialty systems, or niche versions of generic POS software, has many advantages. The software may already be coded with useful merchandise categories, for example. It is often quicker and easier to get started with specialty POS software than it is to have to customize a system from scratch.

A quick Internet search for the type of store and "point of sale" should provide some idea of what options are available. Consider contacting similar stores in other areas to see what they use.

Common Features

POS systems can be purchased supporting a wide variety of functions. Consider which of the following will be needed for the business:

- ✓ Finding items and prices
- ✓ Inventory tracking
- ✓ Multiple payment options
- ✓ Customer information
- ✓ Accounting reports
- ✓ Buyer reward programs
- ✓ Taxes
- ✓ Gift card processing
- ✓ Returns
- ✓ Customization
- ✓ Layaways
- ✓ Barcode scanning
- ✓ Employee records management

What Hardware Will You Need?

Computer

A computer will be needed to run POS software. Different systems have different hardware requirements, so do not purchase a computer until a POS package has been selected.

Printer

A printer is required to print out receipts and credit card slips.

Cash Drawer

Cash drawers allow you to organize the cash, checks and credit card slips you collect during sales transactions.

Keyboard

Keyboards are one way for employees to enter information into the POS system. Another type of input device is the touch screen. If a keyboard is chosen, which is the less expensive but also less intuitive and versatile option, a standard computer keyboard, a smaller keypad, or a keyboard fitted with a credit card reader can be purchased.

Touch Screens

Touch screens are often easier to use and customize than keyboards. If it can be afforded, use a flat-screen LCD monitor. They will take up less counter space, last longer, and use less electricity than the older CRT models.

Scanners

Scanners are used to read the barcode on merchandise and send the product description and price to the POS system.

Check Readers

Check readers can help prevent bad debt by automatically verifying account information. Checks are becoming less popular as a method of payment in the retail world as a whole. However, if they remain popular with customers in a store, a check reader might be a good investment.

Buying Versus Leasing

Very few POS vendors lease their systems. It much more common to finance the purchase through the supplier or using a bank loan when unable to buy the equipment outright. Used systems are available starting at about $1,500. However, these may not provide access to technical support or installation and customization services. New, fully installed and customized systems can be purchased for about $2,500 to $6,000 per terminal.

Gathering Customer Information

To build a retail business on a large group of repeat customers, some way of collecting and organizing customer information will be needed. That way, monthly promotional flyers can be mailed to all regular shoppers or a select few can be e-mailed when a particular piece of merchandise becomes available.

Many POS systems include customer information databases. When using one that does, collect some personal information from shoppers. Many customers are becoming increasingly uncomfortable giving out their telephone numbers and addresses. Train employees to collect information professionally and politely. Customers are often more willing to cooperate if there is some benefit for them. These benefits might include:

- ✓ Invitations to special events
- ✓ Coupons and samples
- ✓ Notification of new products
- ✓ Subscription to company newsletter

Never make customers feel bad about not wanting to reveal their personal information. Instead, stress the benefits of sharing at least their address or e-mail address.

PROCESSING CREDIT CARD TRANSACTIONS

Whether operating a traditional store or a retail Web site, being able to accept credit card payments can increase revenue.

Benefits

Paying with a credit card makes customers feel more secure about the transaction, so they are more likely to make a purchase. Furthermore, many shoppers feel awkward about paying only a small amount with a credit card, so they are more likely to spend more.

As debit cards become more popular, fewer shoppers are carrying cash. If a store does not accept credit cards, it may be losing a large part of the target market.

Costs

The cost of being able to process credit card transactions will vary depending on the plan chosen and the company that is being worked with.

Usually, a one-time fee for equipment and initial programming must be paid. In addition, there may be a monthly or annual fee to cover Internet processing, customer support, and other services.

On top of that, the business will be responsible for paying a "discount rate" of 1.5 percent to 3 percent of every transaction. There may also be an additional transaction fee of up to 50 cents.

Options

These costs can add up very quickly, so it is important to work with a company that will agree to and uphold a reasonable contract.

When looking for credit card processing services, there are three main choices:

- ✓ **Credit card companies:** *American Express* and *Discover* will often contract directly with businesses to provide merchant processing services.

- ✓ **Banks:** The bank that handles the checking account or business loan may also offer merchant accounts.

- ✓ **Independent Sales Organizations (ISOs):** ISOs can also provide merchant accounts and often have less stringent application requirements than banks. Many ISOs are Internet-based.

Whoever is chosen to service the credit card processing needs, be sure to read the contract carefully and be aware of any charges that can be expected. Review and double-check all of the statements carefully.

BUYING HARDWARE

Whether a business chooses to use a POS system or organize transactions manually, a computer will be needed to run business applications.

Where to Buy Hardware

There are many places to buy a computer system, including business supply warehouses, retail electronics stores, and online computer manufacturers. Large companies such as *Dell*™ and *Gateway*® often run special discount promotions for small businesses. However, better service may be provided by a smaller, local store. If planning to buy more than one system, be sure and let the salesperson know. There may be a discounted bulk rate.

There are often better deals on peripherals, such as external hard drives and printers, if they are purchased separately from the computer. Research what is needed, then shop around at retail discounters like **NewEgg.com** and business-to-business specialists such as *CDW*®.

What Do You Need?

Technology capabilities seem to be expanding every day. A top-of-the-line machine can be quite costly. Fortunately, most retail businesses do not need the fastest, most expensive computer.

Before buying a computer, make sure that the POS system requirements are understood. For most business software, more RAM will be needed rather than increased processor speed. Even if the fastest processor cannot be purchased, be sure to have a current generation one and plenty of RAM. A sales representative can help identify the minimum RAM, processor speed, and hard drive size that will be needed.

In addition, keep in mind what peripherals will be used. Older dot matrix printers, which are very handy when printing on carbon copy forms, may require non-standard plugs.

Also start looking at the software applications that will be run. Make sure any system purchased meets the technology requirements.

How Much Can You Afford?

Check the budget carefully before configuring a computer. It is easy to get carried away picking out the latest gadgets. Even when looking at a system that comes pre-configured, some features can be downgraded in order to reduce the final price.

If there is a very tight budget and high technical requirements, consider purchasing a used or refurbished system. When bought through the manufacturer, these will often come with a warranty and technical support.

As new versions of software become available, it might be found that the current computer system does not have the power to keep up. In order to keep up with technology, make sure any system that is bought is upgradeable — the cheapest ones often are not. To help ensure that the computer has room to grow, make sure it has at least some of the following:

✓ Expansion slots

✓ Empty memory slots

✓ Extra drive bays

✓ Large case

Be careful buying the cheapest computer system. Often they are not durable enough to stand up to business use and lack expansion capabilities.

BUYING SOFTWARE

Along with a hardware system, computer applications, or software, will need to be purchased to help increase the business's productivity.

Many computer retailers offer packages of software bundled with the system. Some have special "business suites" which include some of the following types of programs:

✓ Word processor   ✓ Inventory control

✓ Spreadsheet   ✓ Invoice processing

- ✓ Bookkeeping
- ✓ Appointment manager
- ✓ Desktop publishing
- ✓ Staff management
- ✓ Contact management
- ✓ Maintenance schedule
- ✓ Service management

If many of the titles in the bundle will not be used, it is cheaper to purchase just the software needed individually rather than the entire suite.

Where to Buy Software

Business software can be found at the same stores that carry hardware: business supply warehouses, computer manufacturers, and retail electronics stores.

When pricing software, be on the lookout for hidden costs. Some programs may require annual licensing fees or mandatory upgrades.

Used and OEM Software

If the technology budget is tight, consider purchasing used for Original Equipment Manufacturer (OEM) software.

Used software is often a generation or two old, which may make it difficult to integrate with other applications on a computer. Some software companies do not allow resale of their products and nearly all manufacturers prohibit the sale of copied disks and CDs. If these products are purchased or installed, there may be stiff piracy or copyright infringement fines.

OEM software are those programs that come bundled with specific hardware. Selling these applications separately from the hardware usually violates the software company's user license. Increasingly often, what is advertised as "OEM software" is actually counterfeit copies of programs.

If illegal used or OEM software is purchased, there may be legal repercussions and there may be no recourse if the software interferes with other applications, requires technical support, or cannot be upgraded.

Educational-discounted Software

Some software may be purchased at a special educational discount. Many people are willing to purchase programs and pass part of the savings on to others.

Taking advantage of educational discounts to purchase software can be tempting, but it is usually not a good idea. Not only does using the software for other than the intended purpose – education – likely break the user licensing agreement, some programs will have limited functionality. Many printers will refuse to print business material that has been created using educational software.

Open Source Software

For small businesses with small budgets, it does not get any better than free.

Open source software is freely available to download, use, and edit. Nearly every type of application a business may need is available as open source. Search engine giant *Google*™ offers a bundle of some of the most popular freeware at **pack.google.com**.

Some of the types of software that is free to download include:

✓ Web browsers	✓ Media players
✓ Photo organizers	✓ Image editors
✓ Antivirus utilities	✓ Word processors
✓ Anti-spyware	✓ Layoutapplications
✓ PDF readers	✓ Spreadsheets
✓ VoiceandIMapplications	✓ Accountingsoftware

Open source software does not have formal technical support to call or e-mail. Instead, there are often communities of users that may be able to help with problems. Those choosing to use freeware instead of buying software will not have the same caliber of reference materials or tutorials to help when getting started.

Freeware seldom integrates perfectly with other software and there may be serious errors in the program that cause it to crash the entire system.

Desktop Publishing

Brochures, newsletters, stationery, flyer... Even before a retail business opens the owner may feel like he or she is making the graphic design consultant and local printer rich.

A good desktop publishing package, combined with some skill and the right hardware, can make meeting print communication needs cheaper and more convenient.

What Desktop Publishing Can Do

By having the tools and skills for basic desktop publishing, a variety of marketing and communication tasks can be accomplished for a retail business, including:

- ✓ Make business proposals and loan applications better organized and more professional looking.

- ✓ Craft regular newsletters to let customers know about upcoming events and promotions.

- ✓ Produce information sheets about merchandise.

- ✓ Create training manuals and procedure guides for employees.

- ✓ Write business letters to service providers and creditors.

- ✓ Make signs to call attention to special prices or features.

What You Need to Get Started

If a computer is already being used for bookkeeping needs, much of the software needed to start dabbling with desktop publishing is also included.

A good word processing program such as *Microsoft® Word* or *AbiWord* will be needed. If there is a business or productivity software package on the computer, odds are it contains a word processing application.

A word processor is useful for writing and editing documents. Although it may have some art and design features, these are likely limited. When using a word processing program, it is often difficult or impossible to resize graphics, enhance photographs, or put elements exactly where they should be. In order to manipulate photographs or graphics, use an image editor like *IrfanView*, or *Adobe® Illustrator®*.

After the text and graphics are ready, a design application such as *Adobe® InDesign®* or *Art Explosion ® PublisherPro™* can help create effective layouts. Most design programs have a library of templates that make it easier to create professional looking designs.

Using a Professional

Taking the time to master some basic desktop publishing skills can save time and money. Quick signs calling attention to clearance items and flyers announcing the employee holiday party are as close as the computer.

There are some tasks, however, that are best left to professional designers. A good graphic artist knows what works and how to make print materials reflect a business's image and make messages clear.

Many print shops employ designers and will give free consultations for regular customers. Even if a person enjoys creating catalogs and mailings, it might be beneficial to get an expert opinion on how to improve designs.

INFORMATION SECURITY

A retail business may gather personal information on many people. A business will need to keep track of employees' social security numbers and pay rates. Whenever customers pay by check or credit card, their account number will have to be accessed.

Business owners are responsible for keeping the private information about the business, customers, employees, and contractors secure.

Legal Considerations

There are many local, state, and federal laws regarding information security, as well as some industry regulations. Unless the business is a publicly traded company or involved in healthcare, most of the federal privacy rules likely will not apply. Consult the state and city business development offices, however, to see if the business is required to take any of the following precautions:

- ✓ Data encryption
- ✓ Internet firewalls
- ✓ Independent security audit
- ✓ Data backup
- ✓ Password protection

Even if not legally required to take specific security measures, it is a good idea to protect information. Even for a small business, a security breach can be very expensive.

The Costs of a Security Breach

If customer, employee, or contractor information is stolen as a result of negligence, the owner might be charged huge fines and penalties, especially if he or she was not following legal mandates.

Identity theft is a real concern. If a customer's credit card is maxed out because reasonable measures were not taken to secure their account information, the owner may be responsible for all or a portion of the bad debt.

If business information is lost, such as financial records, customer lists, or employee time reports, productivity may grind to a halt while the data is gathered.

One of the most devastating costs of a security breach can come from the loss of consumer trust. If someone finds a printout of employees' social security numbers or customers' telephone numbers in the dumpster, and that leak becomes public knowledge, customers may be less likely to trust the business with their personal and financial information. This bad publicity can be hard to overcome, and profit levels may drop in response.

Types of Security

Despite the possible costs of poor information security, many entrepreneurs do not even consider this vital aspect of business ownership. Some think it cannot happen to them or believe that security is too much of a resource drain. Security does not have to be expensive, but it does need to be carefully planned.

Administrative

A business's first level of defense is the policies and procedures that are dictated. There should be very strict guidelines about who can access the POS system, employee records, and financial statements. Holding to these policies can help reduce the chance of accidental security breaches or malicious attacks by employees.

Physical

When people think of data security they tend to picture computer-savvy hackers busting into encrypted systems. However, in 2006, the *Ponemon Institute* discovered that about 75 percent of data losses came from failing to secure physical parts of the information chain.

By taking a few easy steps, a business's chance of a data breach can be greatly reduced. Physical security measures include:

✓ Shredding unneeded documents, statements, and reports.

✓ Securing backup copies of records in a safe.

✓ Keeping all computers, CDs, disks, and tapes on the premises.

✓   Locking the business office when not in use.

Although it may be tempting to take a laptop to the coffee shop across the street in order to complete bookkeeping or payroll, this may be a dangerous habit. The *Ponemon Institute* study found that lost portable devices caused 49 percent of security incidents.

Technological

Technological security measures include password protecting the system, encrypting data, scanning for computer viruses, and installing firewalls.

Check with the POS system or Internet service provider to see if they offer security applications that will meet the business's needs. In addition, there are many off the shelf security software packages designed specifically for small businesses. Before purchasing, review any applicable legal regulations and make sure that the choice meets the minimum requirements.

For those that have a particularly complicated business information system or handle extremely sensitive data, consider consulting a computer security professional to discuss designing a system to meet the company's needs.

CASE STUDY: LORINDA COLLINS

Lorinda Collins sells weight loss, nutritional supplements, and skin care products through her online business.

"I guess the best thing is meeting new people all the time," says Lorinda.

"The worst part is the money you have to spend without the guarantee of any return. My advice for new business owners is to always be patient. Your business will take off; it just takes time and dedication on your part.

"Just be honest and grateful to every person you come in contact with. You have to be committed to your product or service. People know if you are not being honest with them and you will see that in your sales. As with any project, you get out of it what you put into it."

For more information, visit Lorinda's Web site at **www.power-pops.com/lmcpops** or call 360-482-0596.

16

MARKETING AND ADVERTISING

Marketing is not something limited to big businesses with swollen budgets. Marketing affects nearly every business decision. Customer service policies are a type of marketing. So are the colors used on a Web site, the ads you run in the local paper, and the charity events a business sponsors.

Understanding and using basic marketing principles and techniques can help push a business to new heights.

POSITIONING YOURSELF IN THE MARKET

It is a competitive retail world out there. Owners have to make their business stand out from online stores, discount shops, and big box retailers.

One way to do this is to create a *position* for a business within the marketplace. A business's position is the little niche it holds amongst all the competing retailers. A business's position is what makes it different.

What Makes Your Business Different?

It can be surprising difficult to identify what sets a business apart from the rest of the retailers vying for the attention and money of the target market. To start, list all the features of a business — they do not have to be huge or important.

Let us look at some examples of features of a hypothetical independent book store.

ARMSTRONG BOOKS: FEATURES
• Will special order any book
• Open in the evening and on weekends
• Will ship books anywhere
• Free coffee while you browse
• Cats roam around stacks
• New and used books
• Children's hour on Saturday mornings
• Can trade used books for store credit
• Gift wrapping available
• Play area for children
• Located downtown

Features are simply facts about a business. If those features can be reworked so that they are of some value to the target market, they become *benefits*.

ARMSTRONG BOOKS: FEATURES AND BENEFITS	
Feature	**Benefit**
Will special order any book	You can have any book you want within days
Open in the evening and on weekends	Shopping hours to fit your schedule
Will ship books anywhere	Do your entire gift shopping in one place
Free coffee while you browse	Relax while you shop
Cats run around stacks	Shop in a homey atmosphere
New and used books	Wide range of books to fit any budget
Children's hour on Saturday mornings	Enjoy activities with family while shopping
Can trade used books for store credit	More buying power for budget-minded customers
Gift wrapping available	Buy, wrap, and ship your gifts from one place. Saves time and is less hassle
Play area for children	Keep children occupied while you shop
Located downtown	Easy walk from professional offices and restaurants

The key to positioning a business is to focus on the features and benefits that set it apart from the competition. Like many independent book retailers, Armstrong Books' toughest competition is the bookstore in the mall, one of a huge chains. Armstrong Books does not have the marketing budget of its rival, nor can it offer as many books as cheaply. A comparison of the store's features can help pinpoint possible marketing angles.

ARMSTRONG BOOKS AND MALL BOOKSTORE FEATURE COMPARISON		
Armstrong Books Feature	**Corresponding Benefit**	**Mall Bookstore Feature**
Will special order any book	You can have any book you want within days	Will only special order books in the Bowkers catalog
Open in the evening and on weekends	Shopping hours to fit your schedule	Open evenings and weekends
Will ship books anywhere	Do your entire gift shopping in one place	Does not ship books
Free coffee while you browse	Relax while you shop	Food and drinks not allowed in stores
Cats roam around stacks	Shop in a homey atmosphere	Just like every other store in chain
New and used books	Wide range of books to fit any budget. Large selection of hard-to-find books. Selection changes regularly	Only new books
Children's hour on Saturday mornings	Enjoy activities with the whole family	No regularly scheduled children activities
Can trade used books for store credit	More buying power for budget-minded customers	No trade in policy
Gift wrapping available	Buy, wrap, and ship your gifts from one place. Saves time and is less hassle	No gift wrapping available
Play area for children	Keep children occupied while you shop	No play area for children
Located downtown	Easy walk from professional offices and restaurants	Located in mall

Looking at the comparison chart, there are many ways Armstrong Books can separate itself from the mall bookstore. By focusing its marketing resources on being seen as a comfortable, friendly place where a customer can stroll around with a cup of coffee while the children play, poking through shelves of books, and taking advantage of value-added services, shopping at Armstrong Books can be seen as a good value despite its slightly higher prices.

There is no such thing as a "good" feature or a "bad" feature. Almost anything can be presented as a benefit to a portion of the population. To illustrate this, let us look at the mall bookstore's features and see how they may translate into benefits for their customers.

MALL BOOKSTORE: FEATURES AND BENEFITS	
Will only special order books in Bowkers catalog	Books not in Bowkers may not be in print. Ordering policies keep you from wasting your time waiting for unavailable books
Open evenings and weekends	Shopping hours to fit your schedule
Does not shop books	Leaving deliveries to company Web site allows prices to be kept low
Food and drinks not allowed in store	Shop in a clean store. Any books purchased will be pristine
Just like every other store in chain	Reputation for quality
Only new books	Book will be in perfect condition, no dog ears, marks, or missing pages
No regularly scheduled children's activities	Shop in a quiet atmosphere
No trade in policy	Only carry new books of the highest quality
No gift wrapping available	Quick service and high quality books at the lowest cost
No play area for children	No screaming kids to interrupt shopping
Located in mall	Convenient location. All shopping can be done under one roof.

Armstrong Books and the mall bookstore are both selling books. At first glance, it may seem like they are going after the same target market and should be in direct competition with each other. After comparing their features and benefits, however, it might become obvious that they are serving different types of customers. Parents with their kids in tow, people looking for unusual books, and anyone wishing to kick back with a cup of coffee, a cat underfoot, and a room full of books may be drawn to Armstrong Books. People wanting to grab a book, check out, and buy a pair of jeans next door without having to deal with a gaggle of preschoolers may prefer the mall bookstore.

The cardinal rule of retail marketing is that products are not really being sold — benefits are being sold. If a business can figure out its position within the market and how its features can become benefits to customers, it will have taken a huge step toward convincing the target market that they need those benefits.

CASE STUDY: CORDELL COUTURE

According to David Raisey of Cordell Couture in Frisco, Texas, understanding a business's target market is a critical component of success.

"With our business," says David, "interpreting the needs of our clients hinges on being aware of current trends and understanding how our product stands out as unique.

"Through the years we have done business; we have developed a great Web site that allows our clients to view our products and then contact us. They are given the opportunity to convey their needs via our information request form.

"When we receive this information, we can discern how to best assist each client and meet their needs. Many have questions that are common among our customers. In this instance, we provide them with a direct link to our FAQ page so that they can find the information they need and proceed with submitting an order."

David recommends that new business owners try to make the sales process easy for their customers.

"Understand your customer. Provide them with simple, yet complete, guidelines about how to complete a transaction with your business. Try to anticipate each client's specific needs and provide direction when necessary. Understand that every contact you make has the potential to become your client. But know that despite your best efforts, not all will become customers."

Cordell Couture sells designer wedding gowns, evening, and pageant wear. For more information, visit **www.cordellcouture.com** or call 972-377-6606.

CREATING AN IMAGE

A business's position is where it sits within the marketplace. Its image is how potential customers see it, especially in comparison to the competition.

"Creating an image" may sound like marketing mumbo jumbo that should be reserved for large retail stores, celebrities, and law firms. The truth is every business has an image. Whether or not the time is taken to create an image for a store, the target market will judge and form opinions.

Even if a business does not take the time to define and develop an image, the market will create one – and it might not be a flattering one.

What Determines Your Image?

In the Armstrong Books example, we looked at two bookstores with very different images. The independent retailer was seen as a homey, relaxed, comfortable place to spend the morning with the kids. The chain store at the mall was seen as a sterile, no-nonsense retailer where people could get in, get what they want for a great price, and get out.

So what kinds of things influence a store's image? Here are just a few of the factors:

- ✓ Décor
- ✓ Signs
- ✓ Policies
- ✓ Inventory
- ✓ Logo
- ✓ Store name
- ✓ Location
- ✓ Customer service
- ✓ Clientele
- ✓ Community involvement

Do You Have the Image You Want?

It can be difficult to determine a store's image, but be assured that if a business has been in business for any length of time, it has one. Even if customers were asked how they see the operation, odds are they would have trouble giving a helpful answer. Image is not something people think about, but it is something they act on.

So how does a business go about gauging its image? Start by taking an honest appraisal of the business and answering the following questions:

- ✓ What kind of customers come to the shop? Gender? Age? Income level? Do they come in groups? Bring their children?

- ✓ How many customers buy something?

- ✓ How long do visitors stay in the store?

- ✓ Are there many repeat customers?

- ✓ Would the owner stop at a store that looked like his or hers?

- ✓ How many hits does the business get on its Web site?

- ✓ Where do the Web site visitors come from? Hint: The Web hosting service should be able to provide this information.

- ✓ How many hits translate into sales?

The answers to these questions can be very telling. If more teenagers tend to wonder into the store than older people, the outside of the store likely creates a trendy image. If customers tend to linger in the store an image of comfort may have been created. Using just one sentence, try to describe how people see the store.

What if people cannot seem to get out of the store fast enough? How about if the majority of visitors to the Web site never even see the merchandise? Is it time to change the image of the business?

Creating or Changing Your Image

Whether just starting a retail company or trying to change how a store is perceived, a good game plan will be needed to create a new business image.

In the last section the business's current image was defined. Now is the time to think about what image is desired. For an image to be desirable, it must appeal to the target market. Here are some examples of images to consider cultivating for different markets – it is by no means a complete list:

Stay-at-Home Moms:

✓ Kid friendly – Moms will not have to find a babysitter in order to shop at the store.

✓ Kid free – Even moms need a break. They might appreciate a place to go to get away from the usual.

✓ Companionable – They may want a place to meet other moms.

✓ High-brow – The market may want a place to talk with others about politics, arts, and current events.

✓ Good value – Families on a single income may be interested in getting the most out of their money.

College Students:

✓ Convenient – Students may not have access to a car.

✓ Inexpensive – College students are notoriously short on cash.

✓ Trendy – This demographic tends to keep up with the latest fads.

✓ Familiar – They may want to be somewhere that reminds them of home.

✓ Welcoming – If they are in a strange, new town, a friendly face will be much appreciated.

✓ Unfamiliar – They may want to bring new ideas back to their home town.

Affluent Professionals:

   ✓   Worth the extra cost – This demographic is often willing to pay extra for premium services or added value.

   ✓   Unique – They usually want something out of the ordinary.

   ✓   High-brow – They want to be reminded that they are intelligent.

There are many images that the target market may find attractive. Some of the images even contradict each other. It is up to a business to determine what image is desired and why it would appeal to customers.

After a desired image is decided on, it is time to start embracing it. Make a list of all the qualities that could relate to how the business wants to be seen.

For example, let us consider the fictional store Deborah's Delicious Designs, which sells bouquets of candy and baked goods. The company's target market is young, single, professional women looking for gifts. After careful consideration, the owner decided she wants the business image to be "unique, fun, and cute."

The next step is to start brainstorming about how to achieve that image.

Let us start with the product. Deborah's Delicious Designs' bouquets use lollipops, cookies on sticks, and ribbons of licorice. They are already "friendly, unique, fun, and cute," but the store can dial up the cuteness factor by packaging the bouquets in baskets, adding stuffed animals, and decorating them with gingham ribbons.

Now we will move to the inside décor. Deborah's Delicious Designs does not have a princely decorating budget, so the owner decides to use a variety of paint. The walls are yellow with a painted border of pastel plaid. The curtains are the same plaid. Miniature tea sets, also for sale, are scattered throughout the display, as is the owner's collection of porcelain dolls. Each display table is covered with a bright square of cloth.

Company policy can also influence a business's image. At Deborah's Delicious Designs, all the employees are trained to be cheerful and friendly to customers. They offer each visitor a cup of tea and a small cookie in hopes of creating the atmosphere of a group of friends gathering for an afternoon garden party.

Deborah's Delicious Designs invites customers in with an outdoor display of an edible bouquet, a table set for high tea, and a chalkboard announcing "the perfect gift." The look is feminine and adorable.

Inside and out, the store reflects its desired image. The choice in colors, inventory, displays, and policies are all "friendly, unique, fun, and cute."

CASE STUDY: HOLE IN THE WALL BOOKS

In many cities, online and chain bookstores have severely cut into the market of the independent bookseller. *Hole in the Wall Books* at 905 West Broad Street, Falls Church, Virginia competes with the huge marketing budgets of the big name retailers by offering products and services that shoppers cannot get at the mall.

"We fill a niche that does not really overlap with any of the new bookstore chains," says owner Edith S. Nally. "We sell some new materials, but we focus on a substantial and comprehensive inventory of proven sellers."

Along with shelves stocked with the classics of suspense, science fiction, children's literature, and military history, *Hole in the Wall Books* offers patrons special subscription services tailored to their needs and interests.

Hole in the Wall Books is open weekdays 10 a.m. to 8 p.m. and weekends 10 a.m. to 6 p.m. For more information about their products and services, call 703-536-2511.

REVISING YOUR MARKETING PLAN

When the business plan was written, an initial marketing plan was composed. As a business develops and grows, this plan should be revisited periodically. The marketing plan is the blueprint for letting customers know about the benefits of shopping at the store. Stay on top of what has been accomplished and what should be the next steps.

The first step in appraising a marketing plan is to reconsider the goals.

Have any of the goals been met? Have any of them become low priorities? What new marketing goals can be set for the business?

Remember, the goals should be specific and measurable. Of course making more money or selling more goods is important, but what will be needed to make that happen? How many more customers will have to come through the door? How much more up selling? Should the amount of time the inventory sits on the shelves be decreased by a specific percent?

After identifying the marketing goals, come up with some strategies to help reach them. Common marketing strategies can be divided into the following categories:

- ✓ **Print:** direct mailings, brochures, and flyers

- ✓ **In-store:** customer incentives, sales

- ✓ **Online:** internet advertising, Web site specials

- ✓ **Public relations:** event sponsorship

- ✓ **Media relations:** press releases, editorials

Producing Brochures, Flyers, and Direct Mailings

Many of the strategies that can be used to reach goals will rely on using high quality print marketing materials. If a sale is being held, let customers know through direct mailings. Sponsoring the latest production by the local theater group? Distribute flyers to tell the community. Brochures are an excellent way of explaining the details of incentive programs.

If the budget allows for it, using a professional graphic designer and copywriter can help make print ads polished. If these services cannot be afforded, following a few simple rules can make results more appealing.

Layout Basics

One of the most common design mistakes novices make is to try to fill up the page as much as possible. The result is usually a busy and confusing mess. The message of the advertisement is lost in graphics, taglines, and shading.

Do not be afraid of empty space – it will call attention to what is added. If the design seems crowded, try including only one picture per page and a nice, simple border.

Messages take on a heavier meaning if they are repeated. Use repetition to make advertisements pop. The following techniques are used by the pros to make their layouts look unified and organized:

- ✓ Use only one font throughout the piece. Alter the boldness and size of the text, but do not use any more than two fonts.

- ✓ Make the picture, key words in the text, and the page border the same color.

- ✓ Add a much smaller version of the main graphic somewhere else on the page.

Another way to make designs look more professional is to add a touch of contrast. Using contrast helps the readers have something to focus on and can call attention to key pieces of the message. Try these ways of adding contrast:

- ✓ Write one word of the headline in a much different font.

- ✓ Reverse the color scheme for one word.

- ✓ Add a large bar of a contrasting color.

- ✓ Divide the page in half. Fill one with a dark color.

Contrast can really spice up advertisements, but it is easy to overdo. Use this technique in small doses. Try to call attention to just one element of the piece.

Full color can really call attention to flyers and mailings, but it can also triple printing costs. One way to keep an advertisement in budget is to use only one or two colors.

One last design element that can help marketing material pop is *proximity.* Proximity refers to how close different elements are in relation to one another. Consider the following example:

New River Bakery
Featuring fresh baked rolls, loaves, and muffins.
Special Holiday Hours
Monday through Sunday 8 a.m. to 7 p.m.
Preferred customers: Preorder your Christmas cookies
December 1, Noon to 9 p.m.
Winter concert and open house
December 15, 6 p.m. to 8 p.m.

There is so much information there that the reader can easily get lost in the events, times, and days. By doing nothing but changing the spacing, we can put related items together and make the ad easier to read and understand.

New River Bakery
Featuring fresh baked rolls, loaves, and muffins.

Special Holiday Hours
Monday through Sunday 8 a.m. to 7 p.m.

Preferred customers: Preorder your Christmas cookies
December 1, Noon to 9 p.m.

Winter concert and open house
December 15, 6 p.m. to 8 p.m.

If even more separation is added, the contents can become even clearer. Do not be afraid of white space.

Write the one or two most important elements of the ad, usually the business name or a special offer, in a larger font so they do not get lost. The key here is to make the difference very obvious, so that there is no doubt it is a design feature. If it is subtle, the result will tend to look like a mistake.

When designing marketing material for a business, keep in mind that the goal is to impart information to the reader. Most people will barely look at the ad. If they have to work to see what is important, they likely will not bother.

Content Basics

It might be tempting to write the body of the marketing material first, and then fit a design around it. Most pros, however, recommend laying the ad out first, then writing copy to fit. This method helps avoid overcrowding the page and cuts extraneous words.

Before writing the content, review the purpose of the advertisement. Try to narrow down the concrete reason for sending out the material; for example:

- ✓ To bring customers to the store on a certain day

- ✓ To convince customers to sign up for a loyalty program

- ✓ To invite customers to attend a program, class, or workshop

- ✓ To convince customers to purchase a specific product

- ✓ To increase the hits to the Web site

- ✓ To inform customers about a location or policy change

After defining the purpose of the ad, write it down for reference while working on the copy. There are three parts of the ad that should refer, either directly or indirectly, to the purpose statement:

1. The headline

2. The body

3. The closing invitation

The headline of the ad should grab a reader's attention and make them want to read more. A good headline can be difficult to craft. It should not be too general or too specific.

ADVERTISEMENT HEADLINE EXAMPLES		
Bad	Problem	Better
Hey! Read This!	Too general	What does your porch furniture say about you?
If you want to learn a foreign language, our books, worksheets, and CDs can help,	Too wordy	Always wanted to learn a new language? We can help!
We have new diet books.	Not attention grabbing	Find out how to keep your resolution this year.
New location in North Baltimore	Not attention grabbing	New store. New products. New deals. Same great service.
New line of toys on sale.	Not attention grabbing	Interested in the "Mozart Effect?" Check out our new toys!
All merchandise will be deeply discounted next weekend.	Too wordy	Save up to 50%!

The body of the ad should also reflect the purpose of the piece. Usually, there is no need to give dates, addresses, and times in the body. Those can be separate elements. Instead, the body needs to convince the readers to do a certain action. Tell them why they should come to a sale. List the benefits of visiting the Web site to them.

Whether writing a newspaper ad or a brochure, keep paragraphs short. Readers are intimidated by large blocks of type. Each paragraph should give a distinct piece of information. In brochures, each idea can be developed a little more fully by providing a sentence or two of descriptions or examples.

Keep the writing simple and to the point. Certain markets may require flowery phrases or highly technical specifications, but no one wants to feel stupid. Write so that the average customer will not need a dictionary.

Close the ad by issuing a direct invitation. Some people will not even read the body of the ad. They will skim the headline, the last paragraph, and the artwork. Do not make life harder on readers; use the last sentence or two to tell them exactly what they should do. For example:

- ✓   Come to our Labor Day Sale and "buy one, get one free."

- ✓   Visit our Web site to learn more about our products.

- ✓   Sign up for our "Signature Service" plan and get free shipping with every order.

Make sure all the important facts are included. How effective is an ad for a "one day only sale" that omits the event date? Make sure readers know where the store is, who the store is, what is being sold, how to get there, when the store will be open, and, most importantly, why they should care. Remember, most of these details can be pulled out as elements separate from the headline, body, and closing invitation. Not only does this make it easier for readers to find important information, but it also allows layouts to be recycled more easily – simply replace the outdated information blocks.

Finally, proofread the ad before it goes off to be printed. After it is written, let it sit a day or two, then give it a careful reading. Have someone else proof the piece, too. If editing ability is a concern, consider hiring a freelance editor or writer to give it a quick glance.

Customer Loyalty and Incentives

Making customers feel special and appreciated can be an effective marketing tool. Building customer loyalty starts with offering a great product and stellar service, but loyalty and incentive plans can also help shoppers feel like they are part of the business family.

In order to create customer loyalty, take the time to learn something about the patrons. This can be as simple as their first name – get it off their check or ask politely. Try to remember to call them by name every time to show that they are valued. If more information can be gathered, such as customers' addresses, the relationship can be continued by mailing promotional offers and special invitations.

Most people are hesitant to give private information to stores. Some may even resent being asked. One way to get more information about customers is to set up a free store club. After becoming members by filling out a simple application, customers can take advantage of specific special offers such as:

- ✓ Buy a certain amount of merchandise, get something free
- ✓ Special shopping hours
- ✓ A percentage off every purchase
- ✓ Free delivery
- ✓ Upgraded service

Consider adding some of the following to the membership applications:

- ✓ Address
- ✓ E-mail
- ✓ Phone number
- ✓ Inventory suggestions
- ✓ Other interests
- ✓ Occupation

After customers' contact information is gathered, encourage them to return to the store by sending special coupons and other offers. Make sure previous customers know what is going on at the store, especially events that relate to their interests or occupations. Knowing more about customers' interests, preferences, and needs can also help a business make better merchandise selections.

Consider granting "preferred customer" status to the shoppers that spend the most money at the store. When someone has a special card, he will tend to feel more like a member than a customer. Give "preferred customers" privileges such as:

- ✓ Free gift wrapping
- ✓ No-hassle check policy

- ✓ Store credit

- ✓ Free layaway

- ✓ Priority workshop registration

Sales

A very common marketing strategy is to have "sales," or temporary periods where some of the merchandise is marked down.

There are many reasons stores have sales, including:

- ✓ To get rid of slow-moving merchandise.

- ✓ To compete with another store's sale.

- ✓ Because it is expected during a particular time.

- ✓ To bring in more new customers.

- ✓ To introduce a new product line.

- ✓ Because the vendor requires it.

- ✓ Because the franchise company requires it.

- ✓ To introduce a new service or program.

- ✓ To spur temporary cash flow.

- ✓ To thank regular customers.

- ✓ To celebrate a new location, new name, new owner, or other event.

Never hold a sale without keeping in mind the purpose. Knowing why a sale is being held will help decide how to publicize the event, what items to mark down, and by how much.

If the purpose for the sale is to get rid of slow-moving merchandise, consider discounting only those products. To answer a competitor's sale consider doing more than just matching his sale strategy. Consider reducing some of the fastest moving items in order to get customers into the store.

If a new product line is being introduced, consider offering a reasonable discount on the new merchandise with the purchase of one of the hotter items. To bring in new customers or reward regulars consider taking a straight percentage off everything in the store.

Be sure to market the sale. Send an announcement to the appropriate customers. If the sale is in celebration of an event, why not send a press release to the local media? Flyers and newspaper ads are also possible marketing outlets.

In most areas, merchandise has to be offered at the "regular price" for a certain period of time before a "reduced price" or "percent off" can be advertised. Be sure to check with the local and state business authorities to keep the sales event legal.

Online Marketing

No matter whom the target market is odds are the majority are connected to the Internet. Kids, teenagers, parents, and retirees all have e-mail addresses and online prowess. Not only can using the Internet to enhance marketing strategies help meet goals, it can also be one of the most economical ways to promote a business.

Web Site Marketing

If a company has a Web site, it should be the first point of information about the business. Upcoming sales, new merchandise, expansion plans, and workshops should all be displayed on the Web site. If there are many recurring events, consider adding a calendar to help customers keep track.

A blog can be a great way to let patrons know what is going on in the store. If the owner, or an employee, has a gift for writing, this can really build up excitement about the merchandise and services.

Put the Web site address on everything that leaves the store. If the site is updated regularly, customers will know they can go to it to see what is new and what is coming up.

If a niche market is serviced, look into placing ads on Web sites related to customers' interests. Some may have free directory listings. Being affiliated with a popular site can help generate more hits to a business's Web site.

E-mail Marketing

If a customer has given a business his or her e-mail address, this may seem like an opening to free marketing and unlimited communication. Before sending a bulk message about the latest sale, be sure to understand e-mail regulations and etiquette.

Before sending any marketing e-mails, make sure that the recipient has agreed to receive them. Do this by having them check an agreement box when their address is gathered, whether through the Web site or through a membership application. Make sure to give recipients a way to opt-out of future mailings. Failure to do so may be a violation of the Internet service provider's acceptable use policy and could cause them to cancel the account.

Internet etiquette dictates that marketing e-mails should not be sent very often. The more that are sent, the more likely customers will just hit "delete." Save e-mails for important news. Invite members of the e-mail list to sign up for a regular newsletter if chatty news about the store is going to be sent.

Most people get a huge amount of e-mail. Most of it goes directly to the trash folder. To maximize the chances of an em-ail getting read, use these techniques:

- ✓ Make the subject line descriptive and enticing, like these examples:

    - ☐ "$20 off your next purchase at In Style, On Discount"

☐ "New, safer tools now at National Woodwork"

☐ "Treat yourself with Home Spa coupons"

☐ "Invitation-only, blow-out sale at Fine Jewelry"

✓ Deliver on promises. If the subject line mentioned a coupon, it had better be inside the body.

✓ Do not hide the message. Save long descriptions for newsletters. In e-mails, just give the facts about the event or the merchandise.

✓ Do not send files. Recipients may be concerned about computer viruses and delete the mail unopened.

✓ Make it clear. Like any advertisement, make it easy for the readers to find the important details.

Search Engines

Many search engines such as Google or Yahoo® will sell keyword-related ads. When users perform certain searches, a business's Web site address and a small advertisement will be displayed. The position of the ad on the search engine and the frequency it is displayed depend on how much a business is willing to pay. For more information about different programs, visit these links:

✓ Google AdWords: **adwords.google.com**

✓ Yahoo!® Search Marketing: **searchmarketing.yahoo.com**

✓ Lycos Advertise: **advertsing.lycos.com**

The results from search engine market will depend on several factors including:

✓ How much the target market uses the Internet.

✓ The keywords chosen.

- ✓ How much money is invested.

- ✓ How the competition is using the strategy.

- ✓ The Web site design.

Some of these factors cannot be controlled, but others will allow for experimentation. Search engine advertisement programs include services to help a person see which keywords people are using to get to the site, how often visitors see the ads, and what percentage act on them. This information can be used to help fine tune the keywords and Web site and bring in more online customers.

Public Relations and Special Events

Is the store new or difficult to find? Does the business need to bring more people to the door? Does the staff need to be reinvigorated? Need an image overhaul?

If the business is in a slump, it may be time to use public relations to jump start awareness and drive up sales.

Public relations, or PR, include any services that are done to make a business look good. Done well, these services may attract media attention, which means free press.

Free Classes and Workshops

If a retail business relates to a hobby, free classes can help get more people interested in the pastime – which can mean more customers. The most popular classes are often those intended for rather narrow audiences, like the following examples:

- ✓ Knitting for Kids

- ✓ Guitar for the Tone Deaf

- ✓ Real Men Decorate

✓ First Steps in Ballroom Dance for Brides and Grooms

✓ Gardening with Arthritis

✓ Gourmet Cooking for Diabetics

Remember, the goal for the free class is to get more people interested in the kind of items being sold, not necessarily to create experts. Make sure that every participant leaves the workshop with:

✓ **A smile:** The experience should be fun!

✓ **A list of supplies:** Let them know what they will need to have if they wish to continue honing their skills. Be sure to stock everything on the list.

✓ **The Web site address:** Let customers know that notes will be posted from the class on the Web site for future reference.

✓ **A schedule of upcoming classes:** So they can expand their skills.

✓ **A coupon:** Encourage them to buy. If a business wants customers to take advantage of their newly developed enthusiasm, make it a one day only offer that they can use after the class.

Not all of the class participants will become regular customers. Some might make a purchase that day, some might return months later, some may never return again. Do not be frustrated if a free class does not make much money. Their purpose is to develop future customers and get the word out about the business.

Open Houses and Holiday Events

Hosting a holiday event can be an effective method of welcoming the public into a business. There are five issues that should be addressed to help make the event a success:

✓ **Music:** Provide some seasonal music to help guests feel jolly.

Recorded music can be used if a license is obtained for its public performance. Consider taking the event a step further by inviting a local school's choir or band. Odds are their parents will come, too.

✓   **Food:** It is hard to resist free food. Catering an event does not have to be expensive. Most people will be delighted with freshly baked cookies and punch. However, keep in mind the image of the business when selecting the menu.

✓   **Atmosphere:** Decorate for the season, dim the lights, and spray appropriate scents.

✓   **Freebies:** The holiday party should not be a sale. Consider not even opening the cash register so that there is no doubt about the purpose of the evening. No one will object to small gift certificates or coupons being passed out. A free drawing for merchandise can be appropriate. Free games and activities can also be appealing.

✓   **Publicity:** Unless they know about it, know one can come. Alert the local media, distribute flyers, and e-mail customers. Remind employees to invite their friends.

When planning an event, keep the audience in mind. Families with small children will respond to different decorations and activities than businesspeople on a lunch break.

Nonprofit Organizations and Charitable Donations

Nothing says that a business is a member of the community more than supporting a worthwhile charity. There are many ways to become involved with local nonprofit organizations, including:

✓   Donate a portion of each sale.

✓   Donate a basket of merchandise for a raffle.

✓ Provide promotional materials for participants of a 5K run or other event.

✓ Sponsor a community event.

✓ Organize a volunteer project and give employees paid time off to participate.

✓ Teach a workshop or give a lecture at a local school.

✓ Allow nonprofit organizations to place flyers or brochures in the store window.

✓ Give a tour of the business to a school group.

It may seem crass to expect benefits from an affiliation with local groups. Most nonprofits are happy to acknowledge a business's help by placing the store name and logo on event programs, monthly newsletters, or even signs. Be proud of what the business is doing! Talk about it on the Web site. Mention it in brochures. Send out press releases. Let customers and potential customers know that the business has a charitable side.

Guest Appearances

The public and the press are fascinated by stars. If a celebrity or expert is willing to sign autographs, give a presentation, teach a workshop, or pose for pictures, potential customers may come from miles away. Remember: the bigger the name of the guest, the larger the geographic area should be advertised in.

The best bet is often to select a guest who is involved with the types of products being sold or would be interesting to the target market. If children's clothing is sold, consider a child development expert. If instruments are sold, how about a musician?

If a well-known author is being hosted, be sure to order several copies of her book. Some attendees may want copies signed. If the guest will be teaching a workshop or giving a lecture, ask beforehand what supplies will need to be stocked.

Hosting a celebrity guest can be expensive, but often the costs can be made up through sales to attendees.

Media Relations

Media relations describe ways to get the media to notice a business and present it in a good light.

One of the best ways to start developing beneficial media relations is simply to get to know the reporter who is most likely to be covering the business's activities. This is not necessarily someone who regularly covers businesses. If children's developmental toys are sold, it could be the life-section editor. If books or CDs are sold, it could be someone in the arts department.

Read the local newspaper, do some research, and pinpoint the most likely point of contact. As soon as possible, call the reporter and offer to meet with her to give more information about the business or to send a press pack to her office. Ask if it is okay to send future press releases directly to her or if they should go somewhere else.

A press pack contains all the background information a reporter might need if they decide to turn one a press release into a story. Make sure to have several press packs on hand and to place a copy on the Web site.

The business's press pack should include:

- ✓ A letter from the owner
- ✓ The company brochure
- ✓ A brief history of the business
- ✓ A list of past and current nonprofit and charity involvement
- ✓ A current calendar of upcoming events
- ✓ A business card

✓   A list of frequently asked questions about the business

✓   Copies of recent press releases

Make sure that the contact information is easy to find. Package the elements of the press pack in the pockets of a folder. Do not bind the pieces together – reporters tend to break press packs down, pass around the different parts, and add their own notes.

Whenever the business has a public relations event or goes through a large change – such as opening at a new location, partnering with another business, or winning an award – send out a press release. Save press releases for big news. If the newspaper is informed over every little thing that happens in the store, odds are the correspondence will simply be ignored.

Most newspapers prefer press releases to be faxed, although it is becoming more acceptable to e-mail them. Press releases are expected to take the following general form:

Contact: Contact's Name
Telephone: Contact's Telephone Number
E-mail: Contact's e-mail address

RELEASE DATE, IN CAPS

MAIN HEADLINE, IN CAPS
Secondary Headline, Using Title Capitalization

Body of the press release followed by three pound signs to indicate the end.

###

Repeat the contact information here.

The following is a sample press release about an upcoming public relations event.

SAMPLE PRESS RELEASE

Contact: Carla Johnston
Tel. 999-999-9999
E-mail: c.johnston@yournewsstore.com

FOR IMMEDIATE RELEASE

AWARD-WINNING AUTHOR TO VISIT KID'S CORNER
Lanceport Medal Winner Alex Cole to Read Latest Book

Popular children's writer Alex Cole will be reading his new book <u>A Spider and His Web</u> at *Kid's Corner* in Manchester on Monday, June 8, at noon. The event is free for the public.

"We are delighted to be able to spend the day with Alex," says *Kid's Corner* owner Carla Johnston. "His Little Curly books are some of our best sellers."

Johnston won critical acclaim with his first book <u>Little Curly's Haircut</u>. His second book, <u>Little Curly Saves the Day</u>, won the coveted Laneport Medal.

"I try to write to children like my grandfather used to talk to me," says Cole. "With respect and delight."

Cole will be available to answer questions and sign books after the reading. All his books and related toys can be purchased at *Kid's Corner* before the event.

Kid's Corner on Canal Street in Manchester sells high quality children's toys, books, and apparel. The store is open everyday from 8 a.m. to 8 p.m.

###

For more information or to schedule an interview, please contact Carla Johnston at 999-999-9999

Op-Ed Pieces

If a store deals in merchandise that is the least bit controversial or newsworthy, the newspapers editorial page can become a great source of advertising...and it is free.

Do not think the retail business relates to current events? Odds are there is some way it does. Consider these examples of hot topics that relate to different stores:

✓ Bookstores

☐ Banned books

☐ Illiteracy

☐ Child development

☐ Censorship

✓ Jewelry stores

☐ Black market products

☐ Mineral mining in developing countries

☐ Counterfeit gemstones

☐ Synthetic versus natural gems

☐ Wedding expenses

✓ Craft supplies

☐ Stress

☐ Family bonding

☐ Activities for children in winter

✓ Health supplements

☐ Obesity epidemic

☐ Nutrition

☐ Childhood diabetes

☐ Diet and exercise

☐ Universal health care

☐ Medicare

☐ Pharmacy costs

- ✓ Gardening supplies
  - ☐ Organic food
  - ☐ Risks of supermarket produce
  - ☐ *E. coli* outbreaks
  - ☐ Stress
  - ☐ Family activities
- ✓ Musical instruments
  - ☐ Arts in school
  - ☐ The "Mozart Effect"
  - ☐ Local bands
  - ☐ Loss of traditional music
- ✓ Pet Supplies
  - ☐ Spaying and neutering pets
  - ☐ Puppy farms
  - ☐ Chaining dogs
  - ☐ Adopting pets
  - ☐ Pet overpopulation
  - ☐ Pet abuse
  - ☐ Funding of animal charities

These are all topics that newspaper readers may be interested in. If a related business is owned, they are topics on which the owner may be an expert.

Take the time to respond to community events and interests by writing to the newspaper's *Letters to the Editor* page. Be sure to follow the publication's guidelines and to mention the store and qualifications. Do not make the letter an ad or odds are it will be rejected. Stay on the subject. Inform the readers and help them feel passionately about the issue.

SAMPLE OP-ED LETTER

Editor,

I was very disappointed in the recent Rockville Area School Board decision to cut funding to the Rockville High School Band. Like many residents, I enjoy the band's performances at Friday night football games. Without the boom of the fight song and the riveting halftime show, the games just will not be the same.

I am also worried about the kids who are going to miss out on a musical education because of the decision. As the owner of *Rockville Music* and former president of the *State Music Store Association*, I am familiar with the statistics that students involved in music are less likely to drop out of school, more likely to graduate from college, and less likely to drink or do drugs.

Why does the school board want to hurt the odds of our children's success?

I have seen children come into my store, surly and irritated that their parents are making them play an instrument. I have talked to their parents about their worries. Where do the kids go after school? Who are they hanging out with? What trouble are they getting into? Many of those same children return months later, looking for a more challenging solo or a special piece of equipment. Their parents are not as worried — they know that their kids are safe and learning at after school marching band practice.

But now, all that opportunity and all the benefits of music are not going to be available to local students.

I urge all readers to contact their school board members and demand that Rockville High School Band be supported this year and in the years to come.

Thank you,
Carla Marquez
Owner, Rockville Music

Customer Service and Policies

How customers are treated — when they enter the store, when they purchase a product, and when they return with a problem — is one of the strongest marketing tools. Nothing will go further to create the business's image and encourage word of mouth advertising.

Defining Customer Service

Customer service is more than just helping a customer find the right product or make a purchase. Customer service includes:

- ✓ How visitors are greeted when they enter the store.

- ✓ How the staff interacts with customers.

- ✓ Staff's familiarity with and knowledge of the inventory.

- ✓ Ease of transaction processing.

- ✓ Staff attitude toward customers.

- ✓ Breakage policies.

- ✓ Suspected shoplifting policies.

- ✓ Public telephone and bathroom policies.

- ✓ Ability of business to meet special needs and requests of customers.

- ✓ Extra services available to customers.

- ✓ Flexibility of staff to solve problems for which there are no written policies.

- ✓ Authority each employee has to deal with a situation.

- ✓ Speed with which questions are answered and transactions processed.

- ✓ Appropriateness of sales advice.

Why is Customer Service Important?

A well-worn bit of folk wisdom is that a customer will tell one person about a good shopping experience and six people about a bad one. With lightning-fast communication on the Internet, it is now more realistic to think that a customer will write on one board about a bad experience – where 6,000 people will read it.

Providing bad customer service is a quick way to lose repeat business and future customers.

Small business owners cannot compete with warehouse chains and big box retail giants on price or selection. Where they can compete, though, is in customer service. Policies and model behavior can be set that put patrons first.

Many buyers are looking for alternatives to shopping at huge discount stores. They are willing to pay a little more for goods in order to be more than an anonymous transaction.

Customer service is one area where small businesses have an advantage over the "big boys." Small businesses are not bound by policies written by executives far removed from the retail trenches. They have the power to throw in an extra product or service. They can move displays to help a wheelchair-bound customer maneuver. They can special order merchandise and arrange for alternative delivery.

For small business owners, stellar customer service can be one of the most powerful weapons against the competition.

What is Good Customer Service?

Good customer service is difficult to define because it incorporates so many different aspects of a business's operations. "Customer service" includes anything that involves a customer. For example:

- ✓ Helping a customer select a present.
- ✓ Checking out a purchase.
- ✓ Processing returned merchandise.
- ✓ Determining if a specific style is in stock.
- ✓ Watching a shopper suspected of shoplifting.
- ✓ Pointing out the clearance rack.
- ✓ Attempting to up sell merchandise.

✓   Explaining a service plan.

✓   Educating about product operation or features.

✓   Informing about related accessories.

Evaluate customer service through the eyes of the customer. A situation may be handled in a perfectly acceptable way, but if it made the customer feel stupid, angry, or taken advantage of, it was poor customer service.

Good customer service makes the customer feel valued. It is a business's job to serve the customers! They should never feel like they are interrupting, wasting an employee's time, or pulling employees away from something important. Customers are the mainstay of the business. They should always feel like the store is happy to meet their needs.

Good customer service makes the customer feel satisfied. If a customer feels he or she was bullied into getting an extended warranty plan, a dress that is the wrong size, or a piece of jewelry that is defective, he or she will not feel satisfied with the transaction.

Good customer service makes the customer want to return. When a customer feels valued and satisfied after a shopping experience, he or she is more likely to return to the store.

Good customer service is not just for brick-and-mortar stores. Taking care of customers is just as important for online or catalog retail businesses. Answer any questions about the merchandise. Ship orders promptly and establish a fair return policy.

Good customer service is not limited to customers. Everyone who comes through the door is a potential customer. Even if he or she is just browsing or wasting time that day, if he or she is treated well he or she may come back to buy at a later date. If a visitor is treated rudely or indifferently, he or she may never return.

Who is Responsible for Customer Service

Everyone in a business has an obligation to provide good customer service.

Remember, this is one of the best ways to differentiate a business from its competition.

Employees' Responsibilities

The staff should treat customer service as if their jobs depend on it. Without good customer service, a business is less likely to succeed in the highly competitive retail world.

Consider incorporating the following "Customer Service Commandments" into employee training. A sample poster of these commandments, which can be printed out and posted in the staff area or behind the sales counter, is available on the CD.

CUSTOMER SERVICE COMMANDMENTS

- Greet every person that enters the door.

- Do not make any assumptions about intent based on a visitor's race, age, gender, or manner of dress.

- Treat every customer with respect.

- Smile often.

- Do not say anything about a customer after he or she leaves.

- Answer any question a customer has. If you do not know the answer, find someone who does.

- Go the extra mile to make sure the customer has a good experience.

- Call customers by name.

- Find a way to make a potentially bad experience end well.

- Be an advocate for customers' needs.

Owner's Responsibilities

Ultimately, making sure a business provides good customer service is the owner's responsibility. These strategies can help improve the shopping experience at the store:

✓   Make customer service a larger part of the employee training program.

✓   Stress the importance of customer relations. Make sure the staff knows it is a high priority.

✓   Empower employees to make decisions.

✓   Educate employees about the inventory line.

✓   Make sure the business is equipped to process check, credit card, gift card, store credit, cash, debit card, money order, and traveler's check transactions.

✓   Model good customer service practices.

✓   Establish customer-friendly return policies.

UNDERSTANDING THE RETAIL CUSTOMER

One of the most important factors that will determine a business's success is how well potential customers are understood. If what brings shoppers in can be pinpointed and what makes them buy is identified, retail success is that much closer.

WHAT BRINGS CUSTOMERS IN

Dozens to thousands of motorists and pedestrians can pass by a brick-and-mortar store door every day. If a retail Web site is actively marketed, potential shoppers will come across the links and advertisements often.

What makes customers pull into the parking lot? What encourages people to visit the Web site?

Merchandise

Many customers will seek a business out because they are in need of the merchandise being sold. This is especially true if niche products are offered. If no one is interested in the inventory, building a customer base will prove difficult.

Image

If two or more stores offer the same products, many customers will choose the one that has the more attractive image. Depending on the target market, an image of value, luxury, rebellion, or hipness might be more desirable.

Convenience

All things being equal, customers will go to the store that is more convenient. Convenience does not just mean being easy to get to, it also encompasses shipping, billing, returns, and product support.

Prices

Some customers may be motivated to shop at a store with lower prices. If the target market responds to a luxurious and indulgent image, however, aggressive prices may backfire.

Services

Customers may come to the store in search of repair, consultation, or other services. Many jewelry stores, for example, also offer watch repair services.

Events

Public relation events such as guest speakers, workshops, or open houses can also draw customers to a store.

WHAT MOTIVATES A SALE

Bringing potential customers through the door or to the Web site is not enough — after they are there the sale has to be closed.

So what makes a visitor turn into a shopper? The specific answer will depend on the individual shopper, but in general motivation can be narrowed down to the following categories:

✓ **Need:** If someone really needs the part or equipment that is in stock, making the sale is usually easy.

✓ **Selection:** Having the right size, colors, and styles is crucial to selling merchandise.

✓ **Image:** Customers want to feel good about spending their money. Give them a reason to buy. Will they get to brag to their friends about having a one-of-a-kind purse? Will they be able to forgive themselves for paying so much for a necklace since some of the money went to a deserving charity?

✓ **Value:** People find it hard to pass up a good deal. Even if someone does not need a new belt, they might leave the store with two if they are on the "buy one, get one free" rack.

✓ **Convenience:** If the customer's preferred mode of payment is not accepted — whether it is check, cash, or credit card — or if too much personal information is required in order to make a purchase, policies may end up costing the store a sale.

HANDLING THE TOUGH CUSTOMER

It is often repeated that in retail, "the customer is always right." That is a good rule of thumb for providing stellar customer service, but of course it is not always true. There may be situations where a customer pushes an employee's goodwill to the extent of taking advantage of the business.

Supporting Employees

It is common for managers and retail store owners to take their frustration over a tough customer out on an employee. If a staff member is berated or humiliated over how they handle a situation, staff morale will be hurt, creating a poor image of the owner and the business, and possibly losing a valued worker.

Employees will not always handle situations the best possible way. Here are some methods to turn a bad situation into a learning experience:

✓ Separate the employee from the situation. Meet the customer's needs and wait to involve the employee until after the customer has left.

✓ Do not denigrate the employee for her actions in front of the customer. Move the conversation on to a resolution.

✓ Create a written plan about how to handle the situation in the future and educate all staff members about the new policy.

✓ Take the employee aside and privately explain how to handle the situation in the future.

✓ Always model good people skills. Handle problems calmly and rationally.

Confidentiality

It is very important that any interactions between managers, owners, employees, and customers remain confidential. If one customer is complained about, even if they are not called by name, others will start to wonder what is being said about them!

In the same vein, a quick way to make employees paranoid and uncomfortable is to complain to them about their coworkers.

Relying on Written Policies

Good customer service involves trying hard to make situations right from a customer's point of view. If a customer's demands or complaints are unreasonable, however, it is helpful to have some written policies to fall back on. These policies will also guide employees in making customer service decisions.

DEVELOPING CUSTOMER POLICIES

There are a number of situations that can occur in retail activities. As more experience with the day-to-day functions of a business is gained, many opportunities to develop company policies may become available.

Some of the most common situations for which written policies may be developed include:

✓ **Returns**: How will the customer who wants to return defective merchandise be handled? What about a purchase that he just does not want anymore? Will they need a receipt? Will the current price be refunded or the price they paid? Will they be given cash or store credit?

✓ **Layaways:** Will customers be allowed to pay for merchandise over time? Will a fee be charged? What if they miss a payment or do not pick up their merchandise?

✓ **Breakage:** A customer accidentally knocks over a vase — will they be charged? What if it was not an accident?

✓ **Suspected shoplifting:** How should the staff respond if they think a visitor is shoplifting? When will authorities be alerted?

✓ **Unruliness:** What will be done if a customer is being too loud inside the store, or if two shoppers get into a fight?

✓ **Loitering:** Will "habitual browsers" be welcomed? What about people who gather outside, and possibly block, the door to the store?

✓ **Returned checks:** Will a fee be charged if a check is returned for insufficient funds? Will that customer be able to pay with a check again?

Formatting, Distributing, and Displaying Store Policies

Store policies should be written so that they are easy to understand and follow, even for the newest employee. Gather policies in a folder or have them bound and make sure each staff member gets a copy as part of their training.

Keep a copy of all store policies in a binder behind the sales counter for staff to refer to as needed. Clear plastic sheet protectors will keep them from being torn up.

Consider posting signs about certain policies where customers can see them. This may keep them from questioning employee decisions.

BREAKING POLICY

Part of the art of retail sales is knowing when to break policy. If a return, bounced check, or breakage situation, for example, involves a particularly good customer, it may be more financially wise to skip the service charge than risk losing future sales.

There are some risks involved whenever policies are broken, including:

- ✓ The customer may feel like he can get away with anything.
- ✓ Employees may become confused about procedures.
- ✓ Other customers may also demand preferential treatment.

CASE STUDY: GRAVES PIANO AND ORGAN COMPANY

Since 1962, Graves Piano and Organ Company in Columbus, Ohio has grown to be one of the largest keyboard instrument showcases and retailers in the country.

According to founder and CEO Paul E. Graves, this remarkable growth is the result of a strong commitment to customer service.

"I really believe in the old saying, the customer is always right," says Paul. "We always stress this principle at our meetings> Deep down in my heart I know that it is not always true but keeping it in mind we have managed to uphold a very fine reputation.

"A company cannot thrive without excellent customer service. Many times we go beyond the call in the terms of warranty or quality issues. A customer would not be shocked to hear us say: 'We're sorry but that is our policy,' or 'We've done all that we can do,' or 'You are going to have to take that up with the manufacturer,' but that does not create loyal customers.

"In fact, I do not permit the use of the world policy when dealing with customer issues. The best salesperson in the world is a raving customer, not a satisfied customer, but a customer who's had a memorable experience. Satisfaction is just not enough anymore; you really have to show your customer that you are grateful to them, before and after the sale."

Graves Piano and Organ Company is located at 5798 Karl Road in Columbus, Ohio. For more information, visit their Web site at **www.gravespianos.com**.

18

SALES TECHNIQUES

A business has a good product, runs gorgeous ads, and treats the customer right. The sales should be pouring in, right? If plenty of people come to the store, but not many people are buying, it may be time to brush on sales skills.

Good salesmanship is a combination of customer service and marketing. Being a good salesperson requires:

✓ **Personality** — Customers should feel at ease.

✓ **Understanding the customer** — A salesperson should have a feel for what the customer really wants.

✓ **Product knowledge** — A salesperson needs to be able to match customers with the right product and convince them that it is the best choice.

✓ **Patience** — Nothing will turn a customer off like a salesperson who seems frustrated that they will not commit to buying.

There are three basic steps to sales. These steps can be used for online or in-person sales:

1) Suggest a product.

2) Respond to customer's objections.

3) Close the sale.

MAKING THE SUGGESTION

New salespeople are often reluctant to approach customers about particular merchandise. While it is true that high pressure sales techniques can be irritating, most customers will appreciate thoughtful shopping suggestions.

Effective salespeople keep their customers' best interests in mind. They do not worry about padding their commission or meeting a certain sales quota; they are more concerned about treating their customers' right.

When practicing suggestive selling:

- ✓ Ask about the customer's needs. Are they shopping for a particular occasion or product?

- ✓ Do not make judgments about what the customer can afford.

- ✓ Present two or three choices at different price points.

- ✓ Be enthusiastic about what makes the choices special.

- ✓ Do not be afraid to point out any related products or services — and how the customer could benefit by purchasing them.

RESPONDING TO CUSTOMER OBJECTIONS

Very few customers will instantly buy any merchandise that a salesperson suggests. Most customers will offer some objection to suggestions, even if they do not voice them.

Customers commonly balk at an object's price. They may say the following:

- ✓ "I can get the same thing for cheaper across town!"

- ✓ "I could make that myself!"

- ✓ "I cannot afford that!"

"I can get the same thing for cheaper across town!"

If a customer claims they can get the same product somewhere else, check the claim out. Prices may need to be adjusted to be more in line with the competition. It is possible that the other retailer is selling a lower quality product. Use that knowledge to stress the advantages of the merchandise.

"I could make that myself!"

This phrase can be heard echoing through craft malls, high end boutiques, and specialty shops everywhere. Consider suggesting another, more unique product just to give the customer a selection, but do not feel bad if a sale cannot be closed with this customer. People that say this are often serial browsers who have no plans to buy anything at the store. "I could make that myself" is their way of getting salespeople to leave them alone.

"I cannot afford that!"

Present the customer with more choices in a lower price range.

Remember to be enthusiastic about every product suggested. Know the inventory and be able to respond factually and with confidence if the customer objects to a certain feature. Treat any objection as a reasonable concern and do what can be done to satisfy the customer. If they do not like the color, can a different one be special ordered? If the right size is not on the shelf, double check in the back to make sure it is not there.

CLOSING THE SALE

Some customers need one last bit of encouragement to actually buy the product. If someone is on the fence about a purchase, it is possible to get them to the checkout counter if the pot is sweetened just a little. Luckily, most customers do not need more merchandise to seal the deal. The trick is knowing what they do want.

If what the customer really wants is understood, closing the sale will be easier. Here are some of the most common things that customers are looking for in a purchase:

✓ **Image** — Comment on how owning the merchandise will make them appear to their peers.

- o "That handbag makes you look so put together."

- o "All the other grandmas are going to be jealous."

- o "That portfolio just radiates success."

✓ **Value** — Let them know the purchase is a good deal.

- o "I cannot believe the price on those books."

- o "You usually do not get this kind of workmanship for this price."

✓ **Intelligence** — Customers want to feel smart.

- o "You were wise to buy this week, while the product is on sale."

- o "Smart move protecting your purchase with the service plan."

- o "I wish I had bought this preassembled. I had a horrible time putting mine together."

19

SUPPLIERS AND SERVICE PROVIDERS

The backbone of a business is the inventory carried. To keep shelves stocked and customers happy, it is important to find and keep reliable suppliers.

FINDING AND SELECTING WHOLESALERS

The Internet makes it easy to find wholesalers for most industries. For those interested in retailing a specific brand or line, contact the manufacturer to find the nearest distributor. Those interested in a general type of product but are not sure which brand or model should be retailed should consider attending a trade show. At a trade show, talk with sales representatives, see merchandise, and collect information.

No matter how potential suppliers are found, keep a record of who was talked to and what information was given. Use the following worksheet (also found on the CD) to organize the information. Have several copies on hand and keep them filed alphabetically in a notebook. Later, if preferred, the information can be transferred to a computer spreadsheet or database.

Prices

It is important to get a price list from any potential vendors. Highlight the line items applicable to the business and stable the list to the supplier's contact sheet. Ask if the supplier offers special pricing on any lines.

SUPPLIER CONTACT SHEET	
Company Name	
Web site	
Phone number	
Fax	
Contact Name	
Contact Phone	
Contact E-mail	
Product Lines	
Minimum Order	
Payment Terms	
Warranties	
Return Policy	
Notes	

Payment Terms

Do the supplies need to be paid for before they are delivered or will the business be invoiced? How long will a business have to settle its account? What is the interest rate if a balance is carried? Can the supplier offer any special deals if the merchandise is paid for early?

Return Policies

Make sure it is understood under what circumstances the supplier will accept returns and how the account will be credited.

Warranties

Does the vendor offer any product guarantees to the business or the retail customers? Is the vendor adding anything (stickers, attachments, decorations, etc.) that might interfere with the manufacturer's warranty?

References

Ask potential suppliers for a list of current clients. Contact these references and ask about their experiences with the vendor. The following worksheet, also on the CD, can help organize the information gathered. Use one for each reference talked to and staple them on the corresponding supplier's contact sheet.

SUPPLIER REFERENCE SHEET	
Supplier Name	
Reference Name	
Reference Phone Number	
Reference Fax	
Reference E-mail	
Quality of Supplier's Products	
Selection	
Speed of Shipping	
Handling of Returns	
Other Comments	

ESTABLISHING AN ONGOING RELATIONSHIP

There are many ways to spoil a relationship with a vendor, including:

✓ Trying to negotiate a price after it has been agreed on.

✓ Not working with them if there is a problem.

✓ Continually asking for quotes, but never making a purchase.

✓ Getting into major arguments over small issues.

✓ Being confrontational.

✓ Slow payments.

Remember, suppliers are business people, too. They need to make a profit on their product. Do not be afraid to haggle about prices, especially if quick payment or bulk orders can be offered, but remember that the final price should be fair to both parties. If a supplier is losing money by working with a business, that business may tarnish its name in the industry and find it difficult to get inventory in the future.

GETTING DEALS

There are fair ways to get reduced pricing from suppliers. Getting deals often means offering vendors something in exchange for a discount. Think there is nothing valuable to barter? How about:

- ✓ **Exclusivity:** Promise not to order from the supplier's competitors for a certain length of time.

- ✓ **Cash:** The vendor may be willing to compromise on price if he does not have to invoice a business or pay the credit card discount rate.

- ✓ **Bulk:** If a large amount of a particular product is needed, there may be a bulk rate.

- ✓ **Choosiness:** Vendors may offer discount pricing if they can select the styles and colors they send.

- ✓ **Advertisement:** If parts or tools are being bought to manufacture goods, display on the Web site or in the store that the products were produced using the supplies from the vendor. Consider packaging the supplier's brochures in shipments to customers.

FINDING SERVICE PROVIDERS

Word processing, layout, and bookkeeping software make it easier than ever to take care of many business functions. Even with powerful technology, there are many reasons to decide to contract out some tasks:

- ✓ Efforts seem amateurish.

- ✓ There is no time to learn new software.

- ✓ Resources are not available to buy the necessary programs.

- ✓ There is not enough time to do it all.

If a business is having trouble keeping the books in order, creating eye-catching advertisements, or focusing the business's marketing efforts, it may be time to call in the professionals.

CASE STUDY: FINDING SUPPLIERS

David V. knows the importance of finding and keeping good suppliers. David sells storage structures across the country and prefers to work with suppliers local to his customers.

Working with new suppliers in distant markets presents some challenges. The first is finding reputable companies.

"I usually find suppliers through the Internet," David says. "I prefer online directories to search engines because it is easy to narrow down the choices and find exactly what you are looking for."

When interviewing potential suppliers, David first tries to determine the expertise level of the salesperson.

"I use a little industry jargon. If they do not really understand what I'm talking about, odds are they are buying the material from another supplier. I'd rather not pay for another middleman."

Between two unfamiliar suppliers, David will usually take the cheaper. However, he is not afraid to pay more if there are quality or service issues.

"If a supplier is constantly getting my orders wrong, I am probably losing any price breaks they give me because of decreased productivity."

When dealing with suppliers, he recommends being patient.

"No matter how much work they do in your industry, they still do not know your business. You're unique in some way."

Graphic Designers

Graphic designs help develop advertisements using layouts and artwork that will get the audience's attention and communicate the message. Designers are trained to use color, placement, and imagery in sophisticated ways.

Along with ads, a graphic designer can help create:

✓ Business cards   ✓ Letterhead

- ✓ Logos
- ✓ Signs
- ✓ Membership cards

- ✓ Brochures
- ✓ Training manuals

Copywriters

Copywriters craft the words that make readers want to put down the ad and race to the store. Use a copywriter to help:

- ✓ Write a direct mailer
- ✓ Write for the Web site

- ✓ Edit business letters
- ✓ Create ads

Accountants

If a business is having trouble understanding its financial records or is interested in ways to reorganize the bookkeeping, an accountant can help. Use an accountant to:

- ✓ Calculate and file taxes
- ✓ Audit the business's records
- ✓ Set up a bookkeeping system

- ✓ Interpret financial numbers
- ✓ Plan financial strategies

Marketing Consultants

In the past, only large corporations used marketing consultants. Now, however, many freelancers and boutique firms are eager to work with small businesses. A marketing consultant can help:

- ✓ Create new image
- ✓ Coordinate departments
- ✓ Design a marketing strategy

- ✓ Analyze trends
- ✓ Interpret sales data
- ✓ Evaluate market position

Attorneys

Consider consulting an attorney anytime the business goes through a major transition; for example:

- ✓ Changing owners
- ✓ Dissolving a partnership
- ✓ Incorporating
- ✓ Moving locations
- ✓ Franchising

FINDING A BUSINESS PROFESSIONAL

If a business decides to work with a business professional, the next step is to find the right one.

Check with neighboring businesses to see if they can recommend the service of a professional. There may be an accountant right around the corner who offers a service package for local companies.

Whether contracting with a graphic designer or an attorney, there are many benefits to using a local provider:

- ✓ **Increased accountability:** The professional will likely want to protect his or her local reputation.

- ✓ **Awareness:** If a local firm is used, that is one more person in the area who knows about the business.

- ✓ **Availability:** If a quick project or consultation is needed, a local professional may be able to fit this into their schedule easier.

- ✓ **Referrals:** If a local graphic designer is being worked with, he or she may be able to provide leads on good copywriters and marketing consultants.

There are also many freelancers and firms that are Internet-based and willing to work with a business despite a wide geographic distance. Using an online provider also has many benefits:

✓ **Cheaper:** Internet-based companies often have lower overhead and can offer services for discounted rates.

✓ **Unique:** If everyone in the town uses the same graphic designer, ads designed by someone else may stand out.

✓ **Competitive:** If the search is widened to the entire world, a wider range of skills may be found.

WHAT IF YOU ARE NOT SATISFIED?

One major advantage of using local providers is the increased level of accountability. If an online company takes the money, provides substandard service, then shuts down its Web site, what recourse will there be?

Whether the provider is Internet-based or in the building next door, if service is not satisfactory, the first thing to do is discuss the situation with him or her. Be sure to let them know the answers to these questions:

✓ **How did the final result fail to meet the specifications?** If a consultant was given free range and little input, he may be happy to redo the project based on better-defined guidelines.

✓ **What can the service provider do to fix the problem?** Do not just berate their skills; try to offer some reasonable ways to resolve the issue. Should they redesign the advertisement so that it fits with the company's color scheme? Do they need to write better instructions for maintaining the tax records?

✓ **What will be done if the problem is not resolved?** Will payment be cancelled or will a partial reimbursement be demanded? Contact the Better Business Bureau? Snub them at the Chamber of Commerce picnic?

If an agreement cannot be reached with a service provider, consider taking more drastic measures, including:

✓ Contacting the credit card company or bank to cancel the payment.

✓   Filing a report with the Better Business Bureau, if the service provider is a member.

✓   Requesting arbitration.

✓   Consulting a lawyer.

Remember, the service provider is a business person. He or she may be willing to work to make the project right, or be willing to refund the money if that proves impossible. For this to happen, ask. Give the service provider a chance to correct the problem before canceling payment and jumping into arbitration.

WHEN IT IS TIME TO CHANGE SUPPLIERS OR PROFESSIONALS

There may come a point when it makes good business sense to move to another supplier or business professional. Some of the reasons it may be time for a change are:

✓   A cheaper vendor has been found.

✓   The focus of the inventory has changed.

✓   The current service provider has trouble fitting the projects into her schedule.

✓   The quality of work or products is no longer satisfactory.

✓   A supplier or service provider that is more local has been found.

✓   There has been a personal disagreement with someone at the other company.

If the reason for moving is concrete and specific – such as finding a lower priced source or one with more favorable terms – give the current provider a chance to match the new offer. If the overall quality of work from your vendor or service provider is becoming increasingly dissatisfactory, talk the problem over with them.

After deciding to make the change, try to leave the current relationship on good terms. After all, if things do not work out with the new guys, a business does not want to have burned any bridges with its previous business associates.

20

EMPLOYEE RELATIONS AND LABOR COSTS

No matter how many hours are invested in a business, if a brick-and-mortar store is operated, odds are at least one or two part-time employees will need to be hired. While an online store may be able to hop along nicely for a while through hard work and any volunteer labor, there may come the time when a seasonal or permanent workforce may need to be hired.

Employees are the face of a business. They will help create the image of the store and market the wares, so it is imperative to keep them satisfied and motivated.

There are many small but thoughtful steps that can be taken to make employees feel valued and appreciated:

- ✓ Thoroughly train them for their job.
- ✓ Prepare a comfortable, nicely decorated break room.
- ✓ Provide employee lockers.
- ✓ Make sure the sales floor is comfortably lit.
- ✓ Stock all the tools they need to complete their jobs safely.
- ✓ Allow flexible scheduling options.
- ✓ Pay more than minimum wage.
- ✓ Provide constructive feedback.

✓   Make sure that the work environment is pleasant and structured.

All these little perks may add up, but compare their cost to the possible consequences of not keeping employees happy:

✓   Unmotivated workers who provide sloppy service.

✓   Negative word-of-mouth advertising.

✓   Increased breakage and loss.

✓   Frequent advertisements to fill empty positions.

✓   Time to train new employees.

✓   Paperwork and unemployment compensation if an employee is terminated.

✓   Lost labor while the new employee learns the job.

According to the American Management Association, it costs the business more than 30 percent of a worker's annual salary to find and train a replacement. Keeping the staff happy makes good financial sense.

Job perks and benefits can go a long way toward helping employees stay satisfied. For more ideas on how to keep quality employees excited about their jobs, check out *365 Ways to Motivate and Reward Employees Every Day – With Little or No Money*, available from Atlantic Publishing (**www. atlantic-pub.com**, Item #365-01).

RETAIL ROLES

There are many jobs to do in a retail establishment. In many stores, a single employee may play several of these roles:

✓   **Cashier:** Handles sales transactions.

✓   **Salesperson:** Helps customers decide on products.

✓   **Customer Service:** Processes returns, layaways, and deliveries.

- ✓ **Consultant/Instructor:** Teaches employees or customers how to use products.

- ✓ **Bookkeeper:** Organizes the business's financial records.

- ✓ **Manager:** Schedules staff, handles difficult transactions or customers, evaluates staff performance.

- ✓ **Maintenance:** Fixes business equipment and fixtures.

- ✓ **Janitor:** Keeps sales floor and staff areas clean.

- ✓ **Production:** Creates products to sell.

HIRING RETAIL EMPLOYEES

Innovative motivational techniques and competitive pay rates can help keep the staff enthusiastic and supportive, but an effective retail team starts with good employees.

Finding high quality people to hire can be frustrating and time consuming, but remember – the employees are the face of the business. Hire the most trustworthy, reliable, and responsible staff that can be found.

How Many Employees Do You Need?

For even a small retail store, it is a good idea to have at lease two people working at all times. This allows an employee to eat lunch, run to the bank, balance the books, teleconference with suppliers, or pack orders to ship while keeping someone available to serve customers.

If that many employees cannot be afforded, consider hiring one person to come in for a couple of hours three to five days a week. That way, there will be set times during business hours when personal and business appointments can be scheduled, errands can be run, and paperwork can be caught up on.

Advertising for Employees

The time honored way of finding potential employees is to take out a classified ad in the local newspaper. This is the first opportunity to screen candidates. Remember, time will have to be spent looking over every application. If there are certain qualities desired of an employee, do not be afraid to put it in the advertisement.

It is important to be honest in the ad's wording. If someone is needed from noon to closing on Mondays only, do not advertise "flexible hours." If there will be heavy lifting, mention that. If the job will be over after the holidays, let potential employees know. Not being upfront about the job will only cause frustration.

At the store or office, have several blank applications available to hand out. Consider posting a copy on the Web site. A variety of job applications can be found at business supply stores or use the basic one below.

JOB APPLICATION FORM	
Full Name	
Social Security Number	
Street Address	
City, State, Zip Code	
Phone Number	
Are you eligible to work in the United States?	
Have you been convicted or plead no contest to a felony in the past five years?	
If yes, please explain:	
Position applied for	
Hours Available	
Monday	
Tuesday	
Wednesday	
Thursday	
Friday	
Saturday	

JOB APPLICATION FORM	
Sunday	
Summary of Education	
Special Skills	
Summary of Employment	
Reference Name	
Reference Address	
Reference Name	
Reference Address	
May we contact your references?	
I understand that providing false information on this application may be grounds for not hiring me or for immediate termination at any time if I am hired. I certify that the information above is true and complete.	
Signature	
Date	

As completed applications are gathered, screen them according to these criteria:

- ✓ **Availability** – Is the applicant available when help is needed? Does he or she live near the store?

- ✓ **Legality** – Is the applicant legally able to work in the store?

- ✓ **Experience** – Does the applicant have retail or customer service experience? Check all references.

- ✓ **Image** – Does the applicant seem like he or she will fit in with the customers and retail environment?

During this initial screening, divide the applications into the following categories:

- ✓ **Rejected** – The applicant is not qualified for the job.

- ✓ **Potential** – The applicant seems to fit the job description and will likely fit in well at the store.

✓ **Maybe Later** – The applicant could do the job, but may not be available right away, cannot work the needed hours, lacks a high level of experience, or has some other red flag on his or her application.

Call each applicant who made the potential pile and schedule an interview.

Interviewing Applicants

The purpose of a job interview is to narrow down a field of qualified applicants and find the best one for the job. Job interviews can be nerve-wracking for people on both sides of the interview. Here are some pointers to help the interviewer and the applicants relax:

✓ **Hold the interview in private** – Limit the number of disruptions and people involved.

✓ **Be on time** – Being late or rescheduling the interview can turn off qualified applicants.

✓ **Do not do all the talking** – Give applicants a chance to talk about their qualifications. This will also provide the opportunity to compare what they say to what is on their resume and application.

✓ **Know the details** – Be able to discuss job responsibilities, wages, hours, and policies.

✓ **Be respectful** – Do not judge applicants or be rude. Remember, even if they are not hired, they may become customers.

What to Ask at Interviews

The most telling job interviews are often those that are more like friendly conversations than press conferences, but it is useful to have a list of questions ready about topics that relate to the job and to the applicant's qualifications. For example:

✓   What characteristics do they like the most in a supervisor?

✓   What do they like the least?

✓   Why do they want to work in a retail business?

✓   What do they like doing in their free time?

For more interview questions and hints about finding out the right information, read *501+ Great Interview Questions for Employers and the Best Answers for Prospective Employees* from Atlantic Publishing (**www.atlantic-pub.com**, Item # 501-2).

What Not to Ask – Unlawful Interview Questions

Federal, state, and local laws forbid asking questions that directly or indirectly address an applicant's race, religious creed, color, gender, sexuality, or national origin. In addition, to be in compliance with the Americans with Disabilities Act, general questions about medical conditions or disabilities cannot be asked.

Remember, it is illegal to ask questions that even indirectly deal with personal issues. For example, a disproportionate percentage of some minorities rent rather than own their homes, so that topic should not be addressed. Some questions *not* to ask are:

QUESTIONS SURROUNDING RACE OR COLOR	
• Are you biracial?	• What is your credit rating?
• What race is your father?	• Are you a minority?
• Do you rent or own a home?	• In which neighborhood did you grow up?

QUESTIONS SURROUNDING RELIGIOUS CREED	
• What church do you attend?	• How does your church feel about the DaVinci Code?
• Do you attend church on Saturdays or Sundays?	

QUESTIONS SURROUNDING GENDER

- Were you once a man?
- How do you feel about working with mainly men?
- What if you become pregnant while working here?
- Are your kids in daycare?

QUESTIONS SURROUNDING SEXUALITY

- Do you have a boyfriend?
- Are you gay?

QUESTIONS SURROUNDING NATIONAL ORIGIN

- What kind of accent is that?
- Where are you from?
- Where are your parents from?

QUESTIONS SURROUNDING HEALTH

- How old are you?
- Do you have any contagious conditions?
- Are you going to miss many days of work?

To make sure the latest federal and local employment regulations are being complied with, have an attorney review any paperwork or questions being used during the hiring process.

What to Look For

There will be quite a bit of time and money invested in choosing employees. When interviewing applicants, look for the following characteristics:

✓ **Maturity** – Will the candidate be able to handle stressful situations?

✓ **Communication skills** – Will the applicant be able to nurture relationships with coworkers and customers?

✓ **Dependability** – Will the applicant be on time? Can he or she be trusted with independent tasks?

✓   **Trustworthiness** – Could the store comfortably be left in his or her hands?

✓   **Motivation** – Why did the candidate apply for the job? Is he or she just looking to fill in some spare time? Does he or she want more retail experience? Need extra money?

✓   **Personality** – Will the applicant be a good spokesperson for the business?

Deciding on a Candidate

After interviewing job applicants, the perfect candidate may be found – one with the right experience, availability, personality, and skills for the job.

If that is the case, the decision is easy. It is more likely, however, that there are several candidates that are right for the job or there are no candidates that seem right for the job.

If several qualified candidates cannot be decided between, there are several options:

✓   **Go with your gut** – Pick the candidate that seems to fit best.

✓   **Hire more than one** – Give several applicants a chance. Giving them only a few hours a week will allow the owner to see them in action.

✓   **More interviews** – Schedule follow-up interviews with the candidates. Invite other employees to join and get their feedback afterwards.

✓   **Job shadowing** – Invite candidates to spend an hour or two at the store during operating hours. Not only will they get a feel for what the position entails, but the owner can see how they handle stressful retail situations.

If the decision is made to hire one or more applicants, call and give them a formal employment offer. Take the opportunity to explain the job description again. Be sure to mention the salary, benefits, responsibilities, starting date, and typical schedule.

Ask the applicant if they want to accept the offer. If they do, confirm their starting date and time, as well as to whom they should report.

Rejecting Applicants

Reject unsuccessful applicants politely and honestly. If they ask why they were rejected, be truthful. The feedback may help them be more successful in future interviews. Most candidates are rejected because there was someone more experienced or they just were not available on the right days or at the needed times.

DEVELOPING EMPLOYEE POLICIES

Business owners with small staffs often think that written employee policies are not necessary. If anything comes up, the reasoning goes, we will be mature enough to handle it.

An employee policy is like a business image — if one is not created, one will be created for the business. Whenever a decision is made about scheduling, personal telephone calls, personal appearance, or punctuality, policy is being set. If it is decided not to mention an employee's routine long lunches, it is being said that they are okay. If one employee is rude to a customer, be prepared for others to follow suit.

Most employees are more comfortable working in situations where they know exactly what is expected of them. Consider writing formal company policies about the following issues:

✓ Switching shifts   ✓ Wages

✓ Punctuality   ✓ Raises

✓ Breaks   ✓ Overtime

- ✓ Benefits
- ✓ Dress code
- ✓ Solicitation
- ✓ Weapons
- ✓ Use of company vehicles
- ✓ Personal telephone calls
- ✓ Computer access
- ✓ Employee discounts
- ✓ Substance abuse

- ✓ Performance evaluations
- ✓ Educational assistance
- ✓ Employment references
- ✓ Disciplinary guidelines
- ✓ Availability for work
- ✓ Work performance
- ✓ Neatness of work
- ✓ Training requirements
- ✓ Vacations

THE EMPLOYEE HANDBOOK

Federal and state regulations say that employees must receive written policies about their job expectations. Organize the employee and customer service policies and have copies bound. Make sure every employee receives a copy. Require employees to sign a statement that they have received and read the manual, and then keep the signed statement in their personnel files.

Atlantic Publishing has several tools to help a business create an employee handbook, including the *Employee Handbook Creator Guide* (**www.atlantic-pub.com**, Item #EHB-CS), which features over 100 policies which can be customized.

NEW EMPLOYEE ORIENTATION

Prepare a short orientation for new employees before they start working. 30 minutes should be enough to take care of the following basics:

- ✓ Tour of facilities.
- ✓ Explanation of company policies.

✓   Outline of employee training process and goals.

✓   Schedule days, times, and outcomes of training.

✓   Complete any employment-related paperwork.

TRAINING A NEW EMPLOYEE

An effective training program serves many purposes, including:

✓   Helping new employees feel confident in their ability to perform the job.

✓   Increasing employees' knowledge in company procedures.

✓   Introducing new staff members to customers, service providers, and other employees.

✓   Letting the employer evaluate the employees' abilities, trustworthiness, and potential.

A task can be explained multiple times, but for most people that will not be as effective as hands on experiences. Whenever possible, show or explain how to do something, and then have the new employee work through the steps. The more times he or she completes the task under guidance, the more comfortable he or she will be when it comes time to do it by himself or herself.

Train new employees about every aspect of his or her job, but do not forget to introduce him or her to the activities that go on behind the scenes. If new sales clerks are being trained, involve them in preparing deliveries or arranging inventory even if these tasks are not part of their job description. That way, employees have a good understanding of how all the aspects of the company work together.

ESTABLISHING A PERSONNEL FILE

As soon as an applicant is hired, create his or her personnel file. Start the file with the completed application. As the orientation and training processes are completed, add the following paperwork:

- ✓ W-4 Form
- ✓ Copy of employee's social security card and driver's license
- ✓ Contact form including:
  - ☐ Address
  - ☐ Telephone number
  - ☐ Emergency phone number
- ✓ Job title, beginning date, and beginning pay rate
- ✓ Signed statement that employee has received the employee handbook

As the employee continues working at the store, collect and store the following information in the file:

- ✓ Observations about problems and positive events through the course of employment
- ✓ Performance evaluations
- ✓ Termination date and reasons for termination

Samples of several of these forms are on the accompanying CD.

EMPLOYEE CONTACT SHEET
Employee Name:
Social Security Number:
Address:
Telephone Number:
Cell Phone:
E-mail Address:
Emergency Contact Name:
Telephone Number:

RECEIPT OF EMPLOYEE HANDBOOK

I acknowledge receipt of the Employee Handbook from _____ (name of supervisor) of _____ (name of business). I have read the contents of the Employee Handbook and agree to follow the procedures and regulations it contains.

Signed:_____

Date:_____

INITIAL EMPLOYEE INFORMATION SHEET

Employee Name:	
Social Security Number:	
Beginning Date:	
Job Title:	
Pay Rate:	
Trained By:	
Date Training Completed:	
Notes:	

SCHEDULING

If a store has been in business for a while, it will likely know when the busy hours are and can schedule the staff around them. If the retail business is brand new, however, there may be some trial and error involved as the work schedule is tweaked to meet the needs of employees and customers.

Most retail establishments hire part-time employees, which are usually paid hourly. It may be cost effective, however, to put managers and especially skilled staff members on a salary and full-time schedule.

Hourly employees are entitled to overtime rates of at least 150 percent their usual wages if they work more than a specific number of hours each week. The federal definition of overtime is more than 40 hours a week, but other localities may have even stricter definitions.

To reduce the expenses of overtime pay, it is a good idea to schedule each part-time employee for no more than 30 hours a week. This gives some wiggle room in case employees need to switch shifts or work longer than scheduled occasionally.

It is also a wise policy to require approval on all shift changes so that it is ensured that no one is nearing the overtime mark.

Making an effort to accommodate employees' scheduling requests can go a long way toward developing staff loyalty and satisfaction. One way to do this is to set up a "request box" where employees can deposit their long-term and short-term schedule requests. Be sure to remind the staff to put their names on any requests.

Many business software suites include scheduling programs. If it is preferred, following worksheets can be used to develop weekly work schedules.

Use the "Weekly Staffing Schedule" and the "Staff Calendar" together. First, note how much staff will be needed at each time on the "Weekly Staffing Schedule." For example, if two employees are needed on Wednesday from 4 p.m. to 8 p.m., note this on the schedule.

Next, write each employee's name and note any requested times off on the "Staff Calendar." Fill in the schedule and calendar simultaneously, keeping a careful eye on how many hours each employee is being scheduled.

After the schedule and the calendar are complete, post them for the staff. Try to have each schedule posted at least two weeks in advance.

WEEKLY STAFFING SCHEDULE							
From Dates:		To:					
	Mon.	Tues.	Wed.	Thurs.	Fri.	Sat.	Sun.
5 a.m.							
6 a.m.							
7 a.m.							
8 a.m.							
9 a.m.							

WEEKLY STAFFING SCHEDULE

From Dates:		To:							
10 a.m.									
11 a.m.									
Noon									
1 p.m.									
2 p.m.									
3 p.m.									
4 p.m.									
5 p.m.									
6 p.m.									
7 p.m.									
8 p.m.									
9 p.m.									
10 p.m.									
11 p.m.									
Midnight									

STAFF CALENDAR

From Dates:		To:						
Employee	Mon.	Tues.	Wed.	Thurs.	Fri.	Sat.	Sun.	Total Hours

PERFORMANCE EVALUATIONS

Performance evaluations can be effective improvement tools. Once a year, pass out self-evaluation forms to each employee. The sample included on the accompanying CD can be used. After these forms have been completed and returned, set up appointments for formal evaluations.

At the evaluation, do not give the staff long litanies of their faults. Instead, talk about the following:

✓   Their perceived strengths and weaknesses (from the self-evaluation forms)

✓   Ways they have improved over the past year

✓   Where they can keep improving

✓   Ways the employee sees for improving the business operations

✓   Ways the employee sees for the owner to help them improve

Performance evaluations can be a productive, even enjoyable process. They provide a chance to see where things are going right. To get the most out of the appraisals, follow these pointers:

✓   Do not be confrontational.

✓   Give the employee a chance to give his or her opinion about his or her work and the business environment.

✓   If changes are needed, outline concrete steps the employee can take.

✓   Ask about the employee's professional goals for the next year and determine if there are any ways to help him or her achieve it.

✓   Keep all evaluations confidential.

Be sure to keep a copy of each performance evaluation and self-evaluation in the appropriate personnel file. They will be useful when reviewing employees for raises or writing letters of recommendation.

EMPLOYEE SELF-EVALUATION FORM			
Employee Name: Date:			
Rate how often the following statements apply to you. A = always, S = sometimes, N = never			
I show up to my assigned shifts promptly.	A	S	N

EMPLOYEE SELF-EVALUATION FORM

Employee Name:
Date:

I understand the responsibilities associated with my position.	A	S	N
I work well with other members of the team.	A	S	N
I do not let personal problems affect my job performance.	A	S	N
I fulfill the responsibilities of my position.	A	S	N
I treat all customers with respect.	A	S	N
I treat my coworkers with respect.	A	S	N
I do tasks outside of my job description if asked.	A	S	N
I keep information and issues about customers confidential.	A	S	N
I keep information and issues about coworkers confidential.	A	S	N
I have a good attitude while working.	A	S	N
I follow service and operational procedures.	A	S	N
I show initiative.	A	S	N
I follow through on assigned tasks.	A	S	N

Notes:

Employee Signature:

Date:

PERFORMANCE EVALUATION FORM

Employee Name:
Evaluator's Name:
Date:

Rate how often the following statements apply to you.
A = always, S = sometimes, N = never

Employee shows up to assigned shifts promptly.	A	S	N
Employee understands the responsibilities associated with the position.	A	S	N
Employee works well with other members of the team.	A	S	N
Employee does not let personal problems affect job performance.	A	S	N
Employee fulfills the responsibilities of the position.	A	S	N
Employee treats all customers with respect.	A	S	N
Employee treats coworkers with respect.	A	S	N

PERFORMANCE EVALUATION FORM			
Employee Name: Evaluator's Name: Date:			
Employee does tasks outside of job description if asked.	A	S	N
Employee keeps information and issues about customers confidential.	A	S	N
Employee keeps information and issues about coworkers confidential.	A	S	N
Employee has a good attitude while working.	A	S	N
Employee follows service and operational procedures.	A	S	N
Employee shows initiative.	A	S	N
Employee follows through on assigned tasks.	A	S	N
Notes:			
Evaluator's Signature:			
Date:			
Employee's Signature:			
Date:			

KEEPING GOOD EMPLOYEES

With the time and expense associated with advertising for, interviewing, and training the staff, when a business finds good employees, they will want to keep them.

The best way to keep high quality employees is to make them feel valued. There are many ways to reward outstanding employees and nurture their loyalty to the business:

- ✓ **Pay increases** – Nothing tells a hard worker that he or she is a productive and appreciated member of the team like a raise or performance bonus.

- ✓ **Achievement award** – Singling out a stellar or improving employee for special recognition can be very motivating. Achievement awards can include "Employee of the Month,"

"Best Sales Day," or "Fewest Missed Days."

- ✓ **Increased responsibilities** – Reward initiative and maturity with a promotion. Consider letting a dependable employee handle scheduling, customer service, new employee training, or inventory control.

- ✓ **More input** – Listen to experienced employees' ideas about decorating the store, streamlining operations, or managing customer service issues.

HANDLING TERMINATIONS

When an employee is constantly late for or missing shifts, rude to customers, or shirking his or her responsibilities, it can be very frustrating.

There are many reasons an applicant who seemed so promising during the interview can become a disappointing employee:

- ✓ **Miscommunications** – Even if the job was described accurately and completely, the employee may feel misled. The owner's idea of "flexible scheduling" may be very different from his or hers.

- ✓ **Ineffective training** – The employee might not know the correct procedures for certain tasks or be unaware of her job responsibilities.

- ✓ **Changing circumstances** – For various reasons, an employee may no longer be available for the hours or days he originally indicated.

- ✓ **Personal issues** – An employee may be having a personality clash with a coworker or supervisor. These rivalries can decrease productivity and reduce staff morale.

When faced with a labor issue, the first step is to talk it over with the involved employee. Try to find out what is at the heart of his or her performance issues. Is there anything that can be done to help resolve the problem, such as retraining the employee or acting as an intermediary to settle any disputes with another coworker? Document any performance-related discussions with the employee and any steps that are taken to resolve the problem.

If nothing else works and it is determined that an employee needs to be terminated, be sure to check the local workers' rights laws. An attorney or the local small business development center can help explain the steps that need to be taken in order to legally fire an employee. Usually, a verbal warning will need to be issued to the employee, along with a written plan for improvement. Be sure to have the employee sign all paperwork and make sure he or she understands that if the situation does not improve by a certain date, he or she may be terminated.

Try to use a bad labor experience as a chance to learn and improve business operations. Make notes about possible reasons why the relationship went bad. What could have been done differently in the hiring and training processes? Do any of the employee policies need to be revamped? Is the store environment one that encourages hostility? What can be done to make the position more enjoyable for future employees?

EXIT INTERVIEWS

It is likely that most of the employee turnover will not be the result of firings. There are many reasons why good employees leave. For example:

- ✓ **Graduation**
- ✓ **Moving**
- ✓ **Parenthood**
- ✓ **Improved financial situation**
- ✓ **Changing family obligations**
- ✓ **New opportunity**

Whether an employee leaves under good terms or is fired, try to schedule an exit interview. The exit interview can help pinpoint what is being done right as a business owner and supervisor, and what can be improved.

Some questions to ask at the exit interview include:

- ✓ What did you enjoy about working here?

- ✓ What did you not enjoy?

- ✓ What policies would you change?

- ✓ What can I do to improve the work environment?

- ✓ What can I do to improve customer satisfaction?

- ✓ How well do you feel your training prepared you for your job responsibilities?

- ✓ Do you think your pay was appropriate for the job and for your experience level?

Encourage the interviewees to be honest about their comments. More complete answers may be offered if someone else, such as another coworker, completes the interview.

21

YOUR CHANGING BUSINESS

Perhaps the only thing that can be said with certainty about the retail business is that everything changes. Tastes develop. Technology evolves. Fads come and go.

There are many events that can spell disaster for the status quo of a business:

   ✓   A major discount retail chain moves into the town

   ✓   Another Web site begins selling nearly identical products for substantially less

   ✓   The company from which a franchise was purchased is linked to a major business scandal

   ✓   A product in the inventory line is found to be unsafe

   ✓   The target market is no longer interested in the niche products being carried

   ✓   A major supplier is lost

   ✓   An economic downturn means he target market no longer has money to purchase the products

None of these examples requires that the doors to the business be closed. They may require the marketing tactics, image, inventory, or business model to be changed, but they can be opportunities for growth. To a large extent, success depends on how well a business can respond to market changes.

ADAPTING YOUR STRATEGIES

Flexible businesses are able to carve out new positions in response to market changes. This may mean creating a new image, developing additional product lines, offering more services, or improving customer relations – anything that makes the business stand alone among the competition.

When a new competitor, changing tastes, or market saturation threatens a retail business, study the situation and answer the following questions:

✓ **Is there any position overlap?** Do not give in to the first knee-jerk reaction. Even if a retail giant moves in next door, if the target market avoids big box stores, the bottom line may not change.

✓ **How much economic impact can be reasonably expected?**

✓ **How long will the market be effected?** Is the business competing against a one time sales event or long-term competition?

✓ **What new position can be occupied in the new marketplace?** How can the business continue to differentiate itself from the competition? Does the image need to be updated?

✓ **Does the target market need to be redefined?** If so, do not forget to learn everything possible about the wants and needs of new customers.

✓ **How can the new position be marketed?** What techniques would be most effective in reaching the target market? Some of the following marketing strategies may already be used. Are there others that would work better?

☐ Print: direct mailings, brochures, and flyers

☐ In-store: customer incentives, sales

☐ Online: Internet advertising, Web site specials

☐ Public relations: event sponsorship

☐ Media relations: press releases, editorials

Research and planning are cornerstones to giving a business its best shot at surviving a significant market change.

CONTINUED FINANCING

As a business grows, financing needs might change. Even very profitable businesses sometimes need financial assistance. Perhaps a building is for sale that would be just perfect for the store. Maybe new equipment needs to be bought to offer delivery services or classes. The cash flow may temporarily be interrupted, and the business may need help making payroll.

When faced with financial difficulties, most businesses look to one of two options: loans or revolving lines of credit.

Loans

Business loans consist of a one time transfer of funds from the lender to the business. The business repays the loan amount, plus an interest fee, in regular payments over an agreed period of time.

Business loans are usually used to finance capital purchases such as real estate or equipment. They are most often fully-secured using accounts receivable, inventory, machinery, equipment, or real estate as collateral.

SBA loans are loans that are partially secured by the Small Business Association. Banks and credit unions are often willing to relax their application requirements if a business is approved for an SBA loan.

Before applying for a business loan, update the business plan and gather information about the purchase that is to be financed – such as projections about how the purchase will increase sales or productivity.

Revolving Credit

A business line of credit can be used if a business is having temporary cash flow issues; for example, if there are many outstanding accounts payables or inventory needs to be restocked before holiday sales.

Unlike loans, a line of credit can be drawn off of several times. The monthly payment is based on the principal balance and interest rate. Credit lines are often used by businesses with highly cyclical cash flow.

Like loans, lines of credit are typically secured requiring inventory, real estate, accounts receivable, or equipment as collateral.

22

LEAVING THE BUSINESS

No matter how much owning a retail store is enjoyed or how profitable it is one day the owner may decide to leave the business. He or she may be bored with the industry and eager to build another business from scratch. Perhaps it is time to retire and leave the stress and work of entrepreneurship behind. Maybe it has been discovered that business ownership just is not the right fit.

There are three general ways a company can end: it can be sold, it can be passed on to heirs, or it can go out of business.

If the business is not being passed on to the next generation, the time and money invested in inventory, equipment, and goodwill may be a valuable asset. Before selling the business, check out *How to Buy and/or Sell a Small Business for Maximum Profit – A Step-by-Step Guide* available from Atlantic Publishing (**www.atlantic-pub.com**, Item #HBS-01). This guide will help set a selling point, walk the owner through the negotiation process, and explain the laws and regulations that govern business sales.

CREATING AN EXIT PLAN

Business owners often neglect to write an exit plan, but it can be just as important to the store's future as the business plan. The exit plan should address the following questions:

- ✓ What is the current liquidation value of the business?

- ✓ How much would be received if the business was sold?

✓ What can be done to increase the value of the business and make it more appealing to buyers?

✓ When does the owner want to retire?

✓ When the owner retires, will the family continue managing the business?

✓ What would be the tax implications of selling the business?

✓ What is the process for leaving the business to an heir?

✓ How much loss is the owner willing to sustain before bowing out of the business?

✓ Who will run the business if the owner is incapacitated? Have the necessary papers been completed to put the transfer plan into effect in case of an emergency?

An attorney and accountant can help advise the owner about his or her particular exit planning needs. Situations change rapidly in the retail business world, so be sure to review and update the exit strategy at least every year.

PASSING YOUR BUSINESS ON

After planning, starting, and running a retail business, there will likely be a healthy emotional attachment to the enterprise. It may be preferable to pass the store on to a relative or business partner rather than selling it to a stranger.

There are many benefits to passing the business on rather than selling or simply closing it. For example:

✓ The replacement can be handpicked and trained.

✓ The previous owner may be able to have a continued or sporadic involvement with the business as an advisor.

✓ It may be easier to keep track of how the business is growing and changing.

✓ Provisions can be added to the transfer agreement that may make the deal unattractive to other buyers.

Of course, there are also disadvantages to this plan:

✓ The tax implications are complicated. A lawyer, banker, accountant, and estate planner will need to be consulted to help minimize the tax burden on the replacement.

✓ If the owner changes his or her mind after promising the business to a family member, it may cause hard feelings.

✓ More financial benefits could have been reaped if the business had been sold.

✓ It may be difficult to handle if the direction the former business is going is not favorable.

Deciding on a Replacement

If the exit plan includes passing on the business, a responsible successor needs to be selected.

Before offering the business to a family member or business associate, consider the following:

✓ How involved in the business is the person now?

✓ Is the person physically and mentally able to run the business?

✓ Will there be hurt feelings if the business is passed on to this person?

✓ Does the person have the ambition to continue running the business?

✓ Is there someone more qualified and suitable?

✓ Can the person manage the business alone, or should there be partners?

Make sure the decision is completely comfortable before approaching the possible replacement. Hinting around, offering the position to several people, and rescinding the deals can hurt feelings, cause mistrust, and decrease workplace morale.

Grooming Your Replacement

Ideally, the replacement should already be involved with the business and at least somewhat knowledgeable about what running the store will entail. In order to give the successor the best chance at success, it may take several months or even years to make the transition from employee to owner.

During the transition period, train the replacement in any aspects of the business he or she does not fully understand. This may include:

- ✓ Negotiating with suppliers
- ✓ Scheduling employees
- ✓ Interviewing and hiring staff
- ✓ Bookkeeping
- ✓ Running payroll
- ✓ Purchasing and organizing inventory
- ✓ Marketing
- ✓ Handling disputes
- ✓ Long-term financial planning
- ✓ Filing state, local, federal, and sales tax
- ✓ Running events

Slowly increase the successor's responsibilities within the business. Not only will this let him or her gain first hand experience running the store, it will also raise his or her position within the eyes of the rest of the staff.

Give the replacement the authority to start making decisions for the company. This will allow her decision-making skills to be evaluated.

Constantly talk to the successor. Understand how the process is going through his or her eyes. Does he or she think she is becoming better prepared for the turnover? What does he or she think he or she needs help with?

Set a schedule for the transfer with transition stages where the owner's responsibilities to the company decrease and the successor's role grows. Set goals for each stage of the process. Constantly evaluate how well the schedule is being followed and what tasks need to be completed.

SELLING THE BUSINESS

Another way to leave the business is to sell it – either to an employee, a group of employees, or an outside party. If the retail company has been built into a strong business with a bright outlook, selling the business can provide the cash to start the move on to another phase of life.

Understand What You Have

Whether someone has approached the owner about purchasing the store or listing it with a sales agent is being considered, it is important to understand the business's precise financial standing.

Most commercial accounting software packages can run the reports needed to examine the business. Alternatively, an accountant can help gather and interpret the data.

Before discussing prices or terms, run the following financial reports:

- ✓ Profit and loss statement
  - ☐ Shows if the business is making or losing money.
  - ☐ Does not show business assets.
- ✓ Cash flow report
  - ☐ Shows where money is coming from and going to.
  - ☐ All discrepancies should be accounted for.
- ✓ Balance sheet
  - ☐ Lists business assets and liabilities.
  - ☐ Can be used to calculate the net working capital ratio, a

measure of how well short-term obligations can be met. To determine the net working capital ratio, divide the current assets by the current liabilities. For example, if the current assets are $45,000 and the current liabilities are $32,000 then the net working capital ratio is 1.4.

☐ A net working capital greater than 1.1 is considered positive. Banks will use this ratio when considering business loans.

✓ Accounts payable report

☐ Details money that the business owes.

☐ Lists when bills are due.

Each of these statements presents data about the company. Together they give a good picture of the store's financial position.

Special Considerations

Selling a business can be complex. An attorney should make sure the owner is aware of what property is being transferred and that all the paperwork follows the agreed on terms.

Consider using business brokers if the time is not taken to advertise that the business is for sale or to interview potential buyers. Business brokers can help prescreen buyers and may have contacts that will help sell the business faster. The usual fee for a broker is ten percent of the sale price.

Taxes

There are many factors that will influence how much will be owed in taxes after selling the business. Savvy buyers will negotiate terms and conditions that make much of the tax burden the responsibility of the seller. Some of the terms of the transaction that will influence the taxes include:

✓ **How the purchase price is calculated** — Assets, goodwill, and consulting are all taxed differently. A seller usually benefits if more of the purchase price is based on company goodwill than on assets or a consulting contract. Buyers benefit if the price is based on assets and future consulting from the seller.

✓ **Stock or assets** — Transferring assets favors the buyers, while a stock sale favors the seller.

✓ **Type of organization** — The tax situation will depend heavily on whether a partnership, S corporation, C corporation, or limited liability corporation is being sold.

To get the best deal possible and to fully understand how the sale will affect the taxes, an attorney and accountant should be part of the sales team.

PREPARING YOURSELF

The successor is not the only person preparing for a major transition. Unless there is a plan to start another business right away, the owner will likely be faced with mixed emotions about leaving the store.

The time to prepare for the new phase of life is before the transfer papers are signed. While deciding on and grooming a replacement, think about the follow:

✓ What continuing role, if any, will be had with the business?

✓ What will be done with the new found free time?

✓ Will the income from the business need to be replaced?

✓ Will leaving the business become a regret?

Time and energy have been devoted to the business. It is natural to feel some ambivalence about the move. Plan ahead for how to deal with the time, responsibility, and money issues surrounding the transition.

Obligations to Your Buyer

When presenting the business and sale terms to potential buyers, be honest.

If the buyer is misled in any way, they may have legal recourse should the business under-perform in the future. Consider having an accountant and a lawyer review any prospectus or circular that is prepared for potential buyers.

Many business transfer agreements include conditions that may affect the seller long after the papers are signed. For example:

- ✓ A non-compete agreement that bars the previous owner from owning or operating a similar business for a specified period of time

- ✓ An arrangement for the previous owner to provide consulting services, often paid, on demand for a period of time

- ✓ A schedule for training the new owner to run the business

- ✓ Seller-financing terms

Be sure it is understood how the sales agreement will effect the previous owner and for how long.

Obligations to Your Employees, Suppliers, and Service Providers

The owner should be the one to tell employees about a potential sale – not the new owner, not the business section of the local newspaper, and not the suppliers. Honesty is usually the best policy in an ownership transfer situation. Rumors, suspicion, and fear can hurt the business.

If the business is being advertised to potential buyers, make sure to tell employees first. Be prepared to answer the following questions:

- ✓ When do you plan on leaving?

- ✓ If the business does not sell, are you going to close it?

- ✓ Will you try to find a buyer that will keep most of the employees on staff?

✓   Will you be available as a reference for your former employees?

✓   Do you plan on remaining involved in the business at all?

After a buyer has been found and an agreement has been negotiated, contact the suppliers and service providers about the change. If there is a close relationship with any sales representatives, be sure to introduce them to the new owner.

CLOSING SHOP

In some situations, it may be decided to simply close the business rather than sell or transfer ownership. If the owner is a sole proprietor and has no employees, closing the business is as easy as liquidating the assets, settling the accounts, canceling the state and local business licenses, and refraining from future transactions.

If a partnership or corporation is owned, the process is more complex. The following checklist includes some of the tasks that may need to be completed before the business is officially closed:

- File an annual tax return and check the box near the top that indicates this is the final return.

- Deposit final federal taxes using IRS Form 8109-B or the Electronic Federal Tax Paying System (EFTPS).

- File the final quarterly or annual employment tax form.

- Issue a final W-2 (*Wage and Tax Statement*) to all employees and a 1099-MISC to all subcontractors.

- File a final employee benefit and pension plan report using Form 5500 (*Annual Return/Report of Employee Benefit Plan*).

- Report W-2 and 1099 information to the IRS using form W-3 (*Transmittal of Income and Tax Statements*) and form 1096 (*Annual Summary and Transmittal of U.S. Information Returns*).

- Report any capital gains or losses using Form 1040 (*Individual Income Tax Return*), Form 1065 (*Partnership Return of Income*), or Form 1120 Schedule D (*Capital Gains and Losses*).

- Report shareholders' or partners' shares using Form 1120S Schedule K-1 (*Shareholder's Share of Income, Credits, Deductions, etc.*) or Form 11065 Schedule K-1 (*Partner's Share of Income, Credits, Deductions, etc.*)

- Contact the state and local agencies to determine what forms will need to be filed through their offices.

- Report corporate liquidation or dissolution using Form 966 (*Corporate Dissolution or Liquidation*).

- Report business asset and property sales or exchange using Form 8594 (*Asset Acquisition Statement*) and Form 4797 (*Sales of Business Property*).

Examples of these forms are found on the accompanying CD.

Notifying Employees

Let employees know as soon as possible about the impending close of the business so that they have ample time to update their resumes and put in applications. Be sure to thank each employee for their time and loyalty.

A business closure can be a very emotional time. Employees may blame the owner if they cannot find another job right away and the owner may be irritated at staff members that leave abruptly for other opportunities.

Resist the urge to take out stress on employees and recognize that they are not being disloyal by looking out for their own needs. Try to handle the potentially tense situation with dignity and continue to respect the employees.

Liquidate Your Assets

A business may wish to sell any equipment, property, inventory, and fixtures related to the business. There are many ways to do this; for example:

- ✓   Hold a "Going Out of Business Sale," gradually reducing the price of the inventory

- ✓   Contract with a liquidation company to sell the inventory and fixtures

- ✓   Contact related stores to see if they are interested in any of the equipment or inventory

- ✓   Contact suppliers about buying back inventory

- ✓   List property with a real estate agent

- ✓   Use an auctioneer to liquidate remaining assets

Settling Accounts

Be sure to settle accounts and cancel long-term agreements with any contractors, suppliers, and service providers. Do not forget utility companies. If money is tight, many businesses will help set up payment plans rather than pursue the debt.

Failing to settle an account may result in fines and even imprisonment. At the very least, if a similar business is opened, a bad reputation may be developed in the industry. Suppliers and service providers may not work with the new business or offer unfavorable terms.

CASE STUDY: THE REWARDS OF BUSINESS OWNERSHIP

Sandra Hudecek, owner of White Tail Acres Yarns and Things, was profiled earlier in this book. Her story highlights the impact of running a financially successful business can have on other aspects of your life.

"I have fibromyalgia," Sandra explains. "I was diagnosed with this condition about four years ago. If you are not familiar with this syndrome, it is characterized by pain, fatigue, and a multitude of other symptoms. At first the paint was not too bad, but it has progressed to the point where I now take pain medicine at all times. I was not working outside the house when this started, but it has since progressed to the point where I cannot work anymore.

CASE STUDY: THE REWARDS OF BUSINESS OWNERSHIP

"I have always been a very active person. I used to enjoy gardening, looking after the house and the husband, and crafts of any time.

"As my disease has progressed, I have had to give up many of my activities (including house cleaning — not sorry to give up that chore!). It soon became evident to me that I could no longer be self-sufficient. Even though I did not have a job, I always knew I had the skills (and stamina) to get one if I needed to.

"This, of course, made me feel positively useless. After my experience with my purchased recycled cashmere yarn on eBay, I decided that recycling yarn and selling on eBay would be an excellent way for me to be productive again. I can work at my own pace and sell as much as I am able to get ready for market. I can also do all of the work involved in a comfortable and relaxed environment and take breaks as often as necessary to deal with my condition.

"I often have sleepless nights (another side effect of fibromyalgia) so I can get up and work in the wee hours of the morning instead of laying in bed wondering if I am ever going to get to sleep. It also allows me to take time off whenever I need to.

"My parents are getting older, so I spend as much time as possible with them on the ranch taking care of the book work. I just pack everything in my suitcase and proceed with business as usual at their house.

"I am certainly not going to get rich doing this, nor is that my goal. My goal is to give myself something to do which is of value to others as well as fulfilling to me.

"I am very blessed to have a very loving and understanding husband with an excellent job. I do not have to make x number of dollars per month in order to help keep food on the table.

"My mother helps with the yarn processing and shares in the benefits since we almost always take her and Dad with us on vacation.

"I find this especially beneficial to my situation because it forces me to get up and get moving and work through my pain. However, running a successful business is extremely fun and fulfilling. The positive feedback I receive on my yarn and the money make it all worthwhile and enjoyable."

CONCLUSION

As a retail store changes and grows, business and personal goals may also transform. There is no single definition of success in the retail business world. Some entrepreneurs will not be satisfied until they have a store in every town in the country. For others, having enough money to retire early is the goal.

Some businesses are launched out of the owner's passion for the product. Others are created with an eye toward selling them for a profit.

Business owners are in charge of defining and reaching "success."

"There is only one success – to be able to spend your life in your own way."

–Christopher Morley (1890-1957)

BIBLIOGRAPHY

Bly, Robert. *The Copywriter's Handbooks*. New York: Henry Holt and Company, 2005.

Brown, Gordon, Paul Sukys and Mary Ann Lawlor. *Business Law with UCC Applications*. 8th ed. Westerville, OH: McGraw-Hill, 1995.

Kendall, Kenneth and Julie E. Kendall. *Systems Analysis and Design*. 4th ed. Upper Saddle River, NJ: Prentice-Hall, 1999.

Kotler, Philip and Gary Armstrong. *Principles of Marketing*. 11th ed. Upper Saddle River, NJ: Prentice-Hall, 2006.

Lauer, David and Stephen Pentak. *Design Basics*. 5th ed. Orlando, FL: Harcourt Brace, 2000.

Lynn, Jacquelyn. *Start Your Own Successful Retail Business*. Santa Monica, CA: Entrepreneur Media, 2002.

Menz, Deb. *Color Works*. Loveland, CO: Interweave Press, 2004.

Nickerson, Robert. *Business and Information Systems*. 2nd ed. Upper Saddle River, NJ: Prentice-Hall, 2001.

Parker, Roger. *Looking Good in Print*. 5th ed. Scottsdale, AZ: Paraglyph Press, 2003.

Pinson, Linda. *Anatomy of a Business Plan*. 5th ed. Chicago: Dearborn Trade Publishing, 2001.

Segel, Rick. *Retail Business Kit for Dummies*. Hoboken, NJ: Wiley Publishing, 2001.

Stoughton, Mary. *Substance and Style* Alexandria, VA: EEI Press, 2004.

Williams, Robin. *The Non-Designer's Design Book*. 2nd ed. Berkeley, CA: Peachpit Press, 2004.